Sparing Civilians

Killing civilians is worse than killing soldiers. If any moral principle commands near universal assent, this one does. It is written into every major historical and religious tradition that has addressed armed conflict. It is uncompromisingly inscribed in international law. It underpins and informs public discussion of conflict—we always ask first *how many civilians died*? And it guides political practice, at least in liberal democracies, both in how we fight our wars and in which wars we fight. Few moral principles have been more widely and more viscerally affirmed than this one. And yet, in recent years it has faced a rising tide of dissent. Political and military leaders seeking to slip the constraints of the laws of war have cavilled and qualified. Their complaints have been unwittingly aided by philosophers who, rebuilding just war theory from its foundations, have concluded that this principle is at best a useful fiction. *Sparing Civilians* aims to turn this tide, and to vindicate international law, and the ruptured consensus. In doing so, Seth Lazar develops new insights into the morality of harm, relevant to everyone interested in normative ethics and political philosophy.

Seth Lazar is Professor at the RSSS School of Philosophy, at the Australian National University. He works on normative ethics and political philosophy, and has published articles on war, self-defence, and risk in journals such as *Ethics, Philosophy & Public Affairs, Noûs,* and *Australasian Journal of Philosophy.*

Sparing Civilians

Seth Lazar

OXFORD
UNIVERSITY PRESS

OXFORD
UNIVERSITY PRESS

Great Clarendon Street, Oxford, OX2 6DP,
United Kingdom

Oxford University Press is a department of the University of Oxford.
It furthers the University's objective of excellence in research, scholarship,
and education by publishing worldwide. Oxford is a registered trade mark of
Oxford University Press in the UK and in certain other countries

First Edition published in 2015
First published in paperback 2020

Published in the United States of America by Oxford University Press
198 Madison Avenue, New York, NY 10016, United States of America

British Library Cataloguing in Publication Data

Data available

Library of Congress Cataloging in Publication Data

Data available

ISBN 978-0-19-871298-5 (Hbk.)
ISBN 978-0-19-886352-6 (Pbk.)

For my mum, Susan Lazar, and in memory of Steve Lazar, my father.

Contents

Acknowledgements

Thanks to the Institute for Ethics, Law and Armed Conflict, at the University of Oxford, and to the Institute of Advanced Studies at the Hebrew University of Jerusalem, where I began researching this book; and to the School of Philosophy at the Australian National University, where I developed the ideas and wrote them up. Thanks especially to the colleagues I have had at each of these institutions, who have inspired me at every turn, through both discussion and example. And thanks to the institutions that have funded my research, especially the Australian Research Council, for their Discovery Early Career Research Award. I presented parts of the book at colloquia and workshops in Adelaide, the ANU, Essex, the HUJ, Leeds, Oxford, Rutgers, Stanford, the University of Southern California, Warwick, and Yale. Thank you to all the conveners and audiences for inviting me to discuss my work with them. At those seminars and elsewhere, many people have helped me develop my views, through comments and discussions. I apologize to those I have missed, but thanks to Mike Barnham, Christian Barry, Saba Bazargan, Yitzhak Benbaji, Eyal Benvenisti, Geoffrey Brennan, Rachael Briggs, Timothy Campbell, Lars Christie, Garrett Cullity, Janina Dill, Antony Eagle, Kenny Easwaran, David Enoch, Kim Ferzan, Joanna Firth, Helen Frowe, Alan Hájek, Niko Kolodny, Gerald Lang, Judith Lichtenberg, Matt Lindauer, David Luban, Lisa Miracchi, Mike Otsuka, Gerhard Øverland, Jonathan Parry, Philip Pettit, Jon Quong, Massimo Renzo, David Rodin, Cheyney Ryan, Matt Smith, Nic Southwood, Danny Statman, Victor Tadros, Francois Tanguay-Renaud, Larry Temkin, Lachlan Umbers, Ben Valentino, Pekka Väyrynen, Gerard Vong, Michael Walzer, and David Wiens. Some read and commented on whole drafts of the book: special thanks to Cécile Fabre, Adil Haque, Anne Gelling, and the OUP's readers. Peter Momtchiloff, at the OUP, was supportive throughout: thank you. And thank you to *Ethics* and *Review of*

International Studies, in whose pages Chapters 2 and 4, and parts of Chapter 1, first appeared. Thanks also to the reviewers and editors for those journals, for their many helpful comments. All my work on the ethics of war has its roots in conversations started with Henry Shue in 2006, and with Jeff McMahan in 2007. Thank you to them both for setting me on this path, and for their encouragement and insights shared along the way. My debts to Lu Barnham and Amos Barnham-Lazar are of a different order and kind; I will not try to sum them up here. But thank you; I love you both.

1

Killing Civilians is Worse than Killing Soldiers

1. Overview

Killing civilians is worse than killing soldiers. If any moral principle commands near universal assent, this one does. It is written into every major historical and religious tradition that has addressed armed conflict.[1] It is uncompromisingly inscribed in international law.[2] It underpins and informs public discussion of conflict—we always ask first *how many civilians died?*[3] And it guides political practice, at least in liberal democracies, both in how we fight our wars and in which wars we fight.[4]

[1] Hinduism: Manu, *The Laws of Manu* (London: Penguin, 1991), ch. 7, vv. 91–3, 137–8; Islam: Muhammad Munir, 'The Protection of Civilians in War: Non-Combatant Immunity in Islamic Law War', *Hamdard Islamicus*, 34/4 (2011), <http://works.bepress. com/muhammad_munir/13>; Judaism: Daniel Reisel, 'The Halachic Duty to Avoid Civilian Casualties', *Jewish Chronicle Online*, <www.thejc.com/judaism/judaism-features/ the-halachic-duty-avoid-civilian-casualties>; Christianity and the broader western tradition: Gregory M. Reichberg, Henrik Syse, and Endre Begby, *The Ethics of War: Classic and Contemporary Readings* (Oxford: Blackwell, 2006), 131 (Raymond of Peñafort), 222 (Christine de Pisan), 248 (Cajetan), 324 (Vitoria), 362 (Suarez), 432 (Grotius), 474 (Christian von Wolff). For a general history, see Colm Mckeogh, *Innocent Civilians: The Morality of Killing in War* (Basingstoke: Palgrave, 2002).

[2] Esp. Articles 48, 51, and 57 of the First Additional Protocol to the Geneva Conventions, Adam Roberts and Richard Guelff, *Documents on the Laws of War* (Oxford: OUP, 2000), 419–80.

[3] See e.g. Anthony Reuben, 'Caution Needed with Gaza Casualty Figures', BBC News Online (2014), <www.bbc.com/news/world-middle-east-28688179>; the Iraq Body Count, which collects statistics primarily about civilian deaths in Iraq since 2003 <www.iraqbodycount.org>; and the International Committee of the Red Cross, <www.icrc.org/en/what-we-do/protecting-civilians>.

[4] Colin H. Kahl, 'In the Crossfire or the Crosshairs? Norms, Civilian Casualties, and U.S. Conduct in Iraq', *International Security*, 32/1 (2007), 7–46. Recent (Libya)

Killing civilians is worse than killing soldiers. This is not a rule of thumb. It is not a guideline to help the hard-pressed through the exigencies of combat. It is an irreducible feature of our moral landscape. And killing civilians is worse than killing soldiers, no matter how just or unjust the cause. Whether you're in the Wehrmacht artillery or British Bomber Command, Islamic State or the Peshmerga, killing civilians is worse than killing soldiers.

Few moral principles are more widely and viscerally affirmed than this one. And yet its foundations are shallow and cracked. This book is my attempt to shore up its support. The first step is to be more precise. I will defend this principle:

Moral Distinction: In war, with rare exceptions, killing noncombatants is worse than killing combatants.

Some clarifications: 'civilians' and 'soldiers' are more euphonious, but the fundamental categories here are noncombatants and combatants. I will use these pairs of terms interchangeably; but I endorse a definition of noncombatant and combatant status informed by international law. Combatants are members of the armed forces of a group at war and non-members who directly participate in hostilities. Noncombatants are not combatants.[5] I will use 'just combatants and noncombatants' for those whose side is fighting permissibly and 'unjust combatants and noncombatants' for those whose side is fighting impermissibly.

Second, I named the principle for the moral distinction between harms inflicted on civilians and soldiers in war. It is inspired by, but differs from, the principle of distinction in the laws of armed conflict, which prohibits targeting civilians.[6] *Moral Distinction* makes

and ongoing (Syria/Northern Iraq) interventions in the Middle East have been provoked by anti-civilian violence.

[5] There are, in fact, two roles for combatant status in international law: to identify legitimate military targets; and to assign the right to use force. I am here interested only in the first of those roles (not everyone who is a legitimate military target has war rights under international law). See Articles 43, 48, and 51(3) of the First Additional Protocol.

[6] This is the ICRC's statement of the Principle of Distinction: 'The parties to the conflict must at all times distinguish between civilians and combatants. Attacks may

a comparative claim, rather than specifying a prohibition; and it covers all kinds of killing, whether intentional, incidental, or accidental. It therefore underpins the principle of distinction and the other core principles of the laws of armed conflict: proportionality and precautions in attack (Articles 51 and 57 of the First Additional Protocol). I say more on this below.

Third, by 'X is worse than Y', I mean 'X is *pro tanto* more seriously fact-relative wrongful than Y'. I introduce each term in this relation below. In brief, it means that, holding constant the numbers affected, the degree of harm, and the aim sought, the objective moral reasons against X are weightier than those against Y. This is consistent with Y not being wrongful at all.

Fourth, I focus on killing, but everything I say applies to other harms as well.

Fifth, I focus on *killing*, not on deaths. My central concern is to show that it is worse to kill civilians than to kill soldiers, not that civilians' deaths are worse than soldiers' deaths. The truth of the first thesis does not entail the truth of the second. I think both are true, and the arguments for the first provide some support to the second, but the first is my focus. Again, more on this below.

Last, *Moral Distinction* allows for exceptions. These will be relatively rare, but they must be acknowledged. For example, prisoners of war and combatants who are wounded and *hors de combat* are still combatants, but killing them is often as bad as killing civilians. The best arguments for *Moral Distinction* will help us account for this.

2. Toolkit

My positive arguments for *Moral Distinction* should be available to all those who care about civilians in war. My ambitions are general. But

only be directed against combatants. Attacks must not be directed against civilians.' Some legal scholars divide this into two components: to distinguish, and to attack only combatants. See Adil Ahmad Haque, 'Protecting and Respecting Civilians: Correcting the Substantive and Structural Defects of the Rome Statute', *New Criminal Law Review*, 14/4 (2011), 519–75.

no argument can do without a conceptual toolkit. I advance mine in the twin hopes that it involves no more theoretical commitments than I need, and that the ensuing arguments could be expressed in a different idiom, to convince those who reject something in their foundations.

Everything starts with rights. Persons have a right to life, which protects their interest in living.[7] Sometimes that protection can be weakened or lost. In particular, when killing someone is a necessary and proportionate means to avert an unjustified threat, for which she is sufficiently responsible, then she is *liable* to be killed and killing her does not infringe her right to life: killing her does not wrong her at all. Killing her is proportionate if the threat posed is serious enough to make her liable to be killed to avert it. It is necessary if no other less harmful means could avert the threat.[8] When someone is not liable to be killed, I will call her *innocent*.

Any theory of liability must posit some degree of responsibility for a threat that is enough to render one liable to be killed. There are two broad approaches. The first is comparative. It says that what matters is simply the comparison between the potentially liable individual— call her Target—and the person whose life can be saved by averting that threat—call her Victim. As long as Target is more responsible for the threat than Victim, Target is responsible enough to be liable to be killed.

Non-comparative theories of liability argue that it is not enough for Target to merely be more responsible than Victim. She must also be responsible *enough*. Perhaps it would be marginally better, from an impersonal perspective, for Target to die than for Victim to do so, because Target is somewhat more responsible than Victim. But that alone cannot make Target liable to be killed, because she has moral status, which protects her against marginal interpersonal trade-offs

---

[7] What makes an entity qualify for personhood is a vexed issue, which I do not address here. For a more detailed account of my theory of rights, see Seth Lazar, 'The Nature and Disvalue of Injury', *Res Publica*, 15/3 (2009), 289–304.

[8] This is a simplification; for more detail, see Seth Lazar, 'Necessity in Self-Defense and War', *Philosophy and Public Affairs*, 40/1 (2012), 3–44.

(this will be a recurring theme in this book). Her status generates a presumption against killing her to save another's life for the sake of realizing a marginally better outcome, which can be overridden or defeated only by weighty moral considerations. If Target is substantially responsible for an unjustified threat to Victim—if she poses the threat herself, for example, or if she culpably contributes to it—that can vitiate her claim not to be sacrificed for Victim's sake.[9]

When an act is wrong, it is morally impermissible. When it is *pro tanto* wrongful, a moral reason tells against it; it would be wrong were no other moral reasons at stake.[10] Normally, wrongful acts have a victim—the person who is wronged. An act can be overall permissible despite being *pro tanto* wrongful, if weighty reasons in favour override the reasons against. Since I focus throughout this book on *pro tanto* wrongfulness, I will omit '*pro tanto*' except for emphasis.

Killing the innocent is wrongful. Even when it is overall permissible as a lesser evil, the victim has a justified complaint against the agent who infringed her rights. Killings can be more or less gravely wrongful: consider the difference between murder and manslaughter, for example. Killing is generally more seriously wrongful than other kinds of harm. For seriously wrongful acts to be all things considered permissible, the overriding reasons must be proportionately weighty.

The wrongfulness of killing is a matter of both *agent-relative* and *agent-neutral* reasons.[11] Roughly, reasons are agent-relative when

---

[9] Some hold a non-comparative view, but think the stakes can affect what degree of responsibility is required—if more can be achieved by killing a person, a lesser asymmetry is sufficient. Jeff McMahan has suggested this view in discussion, and it is implied in Jeff McMahan, *Killing in War* (Oxford: OUP, 2009), 227.

[10] I understand reasons as simply considerations that count in favour of or against some action or proposition.

[11] The agent-relative/agent-neutral distinction was popularized in: Thomas Nagel, *The View from Nowhere* (Oxford: OUP, 1986), 152; Derek Parfit, *Reasons and Persons* (Oxford: Clarendon Press, 1984), 104; Philip Pettit, 'Universalizability without Utilitarianism', *Mind*, 96/381 (1987), 75. My own understanding is informed primarily by David McNaughton and Piers Rawling, 'Agent-Relativity and the Doing-Happening Distinction', *Philosophical Studies: An International Journal for Philosophy in the Analytic Tradition*, 63/2 (1991), 167–85; David McNaughton and Piers Rawling, 'Value and Agent-Relative Reasons', *Utilitas*, 7/1 (1995), 31–47; Douglas W. Portmore, 'McNaughton

they apply specifically to the agent; they are agent-neutral when they are reasons for everyone. We all have agent-neutral reasons to prevent innocent deaths. But we have agent-relative *as well as* agent-neutral reasons not to kill. This is why 'killing civilians is worse than killing soldiers' is not equivalent to 'civilians' deaths are worse than soldiers' deaths'. My arguments in this book focus on agent-relative reasons, though they all give grounds as well for thinking that killing civilians is agent-neutrally worse than killing soldiers.

An act can be wrongful in at least three senses.[12] It is *fact-relative wrongful* if it is wrongful in light of all the non-moral facts.[13] It is *evidence-relative wrongful* if it is wrongful in light of the agent's evidence. And it is *belief-relative wrongful* if it is wrongful in light of the agent's beliefs. I will use 'fact-relative' and 'objective' interchangeably, and employ 'subjective' as an umbrella term to cover 'evidence-relative' and 'belief-relative' wrongfulness. In this book I focus on objective wrongfulness.

3. Why Moral Distinction Matters

The laws of armed conflict protect civilians through the principles of noncombatant immunity (also known as the principle of distinction), proportionality, and precautions in attack. These are most influentially articulated in the First Additional Protocol to the Geneva conventions.[14] Noncombatant immunity protects civilians against intentional attack (e.g. Article 48). Proportionality protects them against excessive incidental harm (e.g. Article 51). Precautions in

and Rawling on the Agent-Relative/Agent-Neutral Distinction', *Utilitas*, 13/3 (2001), 350–6.

[12] This terminology was introduced by Derek Parfit, *On What Matters* (Oxford: OUP, 2011), ch. 7. See also Victor Tadros, *The Ends of Harm: The Moral Foundations of Criminal Law* (Oxford: OUP, 2011), ch. 10.

[13] Parfit writes that an act is '*wrong* in the *fact-relative* sense just when this act would be wrong in the ordinary sense if we knew all of the morally relevant facts' (Parfit, *On What Matters*, 150). However, what matters is not whether we know the facts, but what the facts are.

[14] See Roberts and Guelff, *Documents*, 419–80.

attack requires belligerents to take measures to reduce the risk to civilians, for example by choosing objectives that minimize civilian casualties, and warning them of impending attacks (e.g. Article 57). These laws, and the norms that underpin them, are under constant pressure. Each imposes costs on belligerents, requiring them to take additional risks, and depriving them of tactical options that could improve their chances of success. Each principle must be constantly buttressed and reaffirmed, so that they hold up when hard-pressed military and political leaders are tempted to disregard them. *Moral Distinction* is essential to that process. If we cannot vindicate *Moral Distinction*, then we cannot endorse any of these more substantial protections. If killing civilians is not worse than killing soldiers, then either soldiers and civilians should enjoy the same protections, making it impossible to fight wars legally, or the standards that currently apply to soldiers should be extended to civilians, legitimating a form of total war. *Moral Distinction* does not entail noncombatant immunity, proportionality, or precautions in attack. But it is necessary to their justification.

Moral Distinction is not only essential to limiting armed conflict. It is also crucial to its justification. Even in the 'best' wars, and certainly in the kinds of morally mixed wars we more commonly fight, we invariably kill many innocent people.[15] If any such wars are to be justified, we must explain how violating some people's rights to life can be a permissible lesser evil. And we must do so without over-generating permissions. In particular, we must argue that killing innocent unjust combatants can be permissible, but that killing innocent unjust noncombatants is not. *Moral Distinction* is a central premise in that argument.[16]

---

[15] Seth Lazar, 'Responsibility, Risk, and Killing in Self-Defense', *Ethics*, 119/4 (2009), 699–728; Seth Lazar, 'The Responsibility Dilemma for *Killing in War*: A Review Essay', *Philosophy and Public Affairs*, 38/2 (2010), 180–213.

[16] For more on lesser-evil justifications for killing in war, see Seth Lazar, 'Associative Duties and the Ethics of Killing in War', *Journal of Practical Ethics*, 1/1 (2013), 3–48.

4. Moral Distinction in Trouble

In *Just and Unjust Wars*, Michael Walzer offered a simple account of the permissibility of killing in war, which translates easily into a defence of *Moral Distinction*.[17] Civilians and soldiers all start with rights to life. But soldiers pose lethal threats, so lose that right. Killing civilians violates their rights; killing soldiers does not, so killing civilians is worse than killing soldiers. In recent years, however, philosophers have exposed the flawed machinery behind this welcome result, and doubt has settled in. Walzer had his facts wrong: many soldiers contribute no more to threats than do many civilians. Worse, his account of how one loses the right to life is mistaken.[18] Posing a threat is neither necessary nor sufficient for one to become liable to be killed.

The critique of Walzer has been compelling; but his critics have proved too much. They cannot explain why killing civilians is worse than killing soldiers. On their revisionist view, one loses the right to life by being responsible for contributing to unjustified threats.[19] Yet, first, this principle does not distinguish between killing civilians and soldiers on the just side (if there is one).[20] Second, many soldiers and civilians are equally responsible for such contributions; indeed, many soldiers and civilians are not responsible at all.[21]

---

[17] Michael Walzer, *Just and Unjust Wars: A Moral Argument with Historical Illustrations* (New York: Basic Books, 2006).

[18] See e.g. Robert Holmes, *On War and Morality* (Princeton: PUP, 1989); Jeff McMahan, 'Innocence, Self-Defense and Killing in War', *Journal of Political Philosophy*, 2/3 (1994), 193–221; Richard Norman, *Ethics, Killing and War* (Cambridge: CUP, 1995); David Rodin, *War and Self-Defense* (Oxford: Clarendon Press, 2002); Tony Coady, *Morality and Political Violence* (Cambridge: CUP, 2008); McMahan, *Killing in War*.

[19] See e.g. McMahan, 'Innocence'; Jeff McMahan, 'The Ethics of Killing in War', *Ethics*, 114/1 (2004), 693–732; Cécile Fabre, *Cosmopolitan War* (Oxford: OUP, 2012); Helen Frowe, *Defensive Killing* (Oxford: OUP, 2014).

[20] McMahan, 'Killing in War', 718; McMahan, *Killing in War*, 16; Fabre, *Cosmopolitan War*, 72–5.

[21] McMahan, 'Innocence': 210; Lazar, 'Responsibility Dilemma'; Noam J. Zohar, 'Innocence and Complex Threats: Upholding the War Ethic and the Condemnation of Terrorism', *Ethics*, 114/1 (2004), 742.

The first point is widely acknowledged by revisionist just war theorists; indeed, they often regard it as a feature, not a bug, of their view.[22] This is a mistake, which the arguments of this book can help to remedy. The second point is more controversial, and bears some elaboration.

We can start by distinguishing between two broad approaches to specifying when one is liable to be killed. A *low-threshold* view allows that some minimal degree of responsibility for contributing to an unjustified threat can render one liable to be killed.[23] A *high-threshold* view requires a high degree of responsibility—for example, that one pose the threat oneself or culpably contribute to it. In principle, these two approaches cut across the comparative/non-comparative distinction I have drawn, but in practice comparativists will typically endorse the low-threshold view and non-comparativists a high threshold.

The next step is to advance an empirical generalization about responsibility in war:

Overlap Hypothesis: A morally significant proportion of noncombatants are as responsible as a morally significant proportion of combatants for contributions to unjustified threats.[24]

By 'a morally significant proportion', I mean that the overlap is not slight enough to yield only 'rare exceptions'. Nor is it a coextension: it is consistent with most combatants being more responsible than most noncombatants. As already noted, revisionists readily concede that killing just noncombatants is no worse than killing just combatants. They should not do so, but set that aside for now: the *Overlap Hypothesis* is true for unjust combatants and unjust noncombatants as well, and that poses a more serious problem for their view.

The problem is this: if we make the liability threshold low enough to ensure that all unjust combatants are liable, we will make too many unjust noncombatants liable as well. If we endorse a high threshold

---

[22] See esp. Frowe, *Defensive Killing*.

[23] Note that one can be responsible for contributing to a threat either through action or omission. On this, see chapter 6. Thanks to Steve Woodside for discussion of this point.

[24] This reformulates my central point in Lazar, 'Responsibility Dilemma'.

of responsibility for liability, then we will find that too few unjust combatants are liable. The first would radically undermine the protection of noncombatants in war; the second would leave us without legitimate means to fight otherwise just wars. And there is no 'Goldilocks' position. If we adopt a mid-level threshold of responsibility for liability, too many combatants and noncombatants will be innocent and liable respectively.

This responsibility dilemma throws into doubt the possibility of fighting a just but restrained war. If the low-threshold view is right, then many of the restraints that *Moral Distinction* underpins would be radically weakened in force and scope. If many civilians are liable to be killed, then they should not enjoy the protections international law currently affords them.

But if the high-threshold view is right, then fighting just wars becomes incredibly difficult. Innocent and liable soldiers will inevitably be intermingled. In the absence of 'liability-seeking missiles', we cannot possibly confine our attacks only to the liable. We must therefore either endorse pacifism (if we think nothing could justify us in overriding so many rights to life) or we must explain why intentionally killing so many innocent soldiers can be objectively justified as a lesser evil. Moreover, we must do so without rendering attacking innocent civilians a permissible lesser evil too, on pain of again endorsing a wholesale onslaught on the protection of civilians in war.

This is about objective justification, not about the difficulty of applying our objective moral theory in the confusing circumstances of war. We are unable to intentionally kill only the liable, and we know this from the outset. If the high-threshold view is right, then we will invariably intentionally kill many innocent people, including many innocent unjust combatants. So warfare can be permissible only if killing those innocents is an objectively permissible lesser evil. But if attacking innocent combatants can be objectively permissible, then why not also attacking innocent noncombatants?

Is the *Overlap Hypothesis* true? It is an empirical thesis, so proving it would require detailed empirical enquiry into the contributions of combatants and noncombatants to their political communities' military efforts. Since individual rights are at stake, we would have to look at individuals' contributions. This would be a mammoth task, and is beyond me.[25] However, some general empirical research is relevant, as are some a priori reasons in favour of the *Overlap Hypothesis*.

First, distinguish between different categories of threat in war. Micro-threats are threats to specific people's lives; the macro-threat is the overarching threat posed by one belligerent to the other—for example, a threat to territorial integrity or political sovereignty. The best argument for the *Overlap Hypothesis* shows that many combatants make negligible, unnecessary, causal contributions to micro- and macro-threats; many noncombatants do the same, and those combatants are no more culpable for their contributions than are the noncombatants.

---

[25] Although notice that many philosophers explicitly or implicitly endorse the *Overlap Hypothesis*. For example, see Richard J. Arneson, 'Just Warfare Theory and Noncombatant Immunity', *Cornell International Law Journal*, 39 (2006), 667; Michael Gross, *Moral Dilemmas of Modern War: Torture, Assassination and Blackmail in an Age of Asymmetric Conflict* (Cambridge: CUP, 2010), 159; Noam J. Zohar, 'Collective War and Individualistic Ethics: Against the Conscription of "Self-Defense"', *Political Theory*, 21/4 (1993), 615; Asa Kasher and Amos Yadlin, 'Military Ethics of Fighting Terror: An Israeli Perspective', *Journal of Military Ethics*, 4 (2005), 13–14; Jeff McMahan, 'Killing in War: A Reply to Walzer', *Philosophia*, 34/1 (2006), 50–1. Empirical research on this topic is scarce, but for supporting evidence, see Benjamin Valentino, Paul Huth, and Sarah Croco, 'Bear Any Burden? How Democracies Minimize the Costs of War', *Journal of Politics*, 72/2 (2010), 531; Alexander Downes, 'Desperate Times, Desperate Measures: The Causes of Civilian Victimization in War', *International Security*, 30/4 (2006), 157–8; Benjamin Valentino, Paul Huth, and Dylan Balch-Lindsay, '"Draining the Sea": Mass Killing and Guerrilla Warfare', *International Organization*, 58/2 (2004), 379. Hugo Slim offers a detailed qualitative discussion of the ways in which civilians have been implicated in warfare throughout history: Hugo Slim, *Killing Civilians: Method, Madness and Morality in War* (London: Hurst, 2007), 148–9, 89–205. Besides the obvious points about taxes and industrial support, Slim writes, 'Social connection offers sustenance of a different but important kind to economic activity in war. If labour can be used to convert economic capital into weapons and supplies, relationships can act to convert social capital into morale. Having access to such social and emotional capital is integral to any war effort. The knowledge that one is fighting for a group, protecting a family or preserving a way of life or a set of beliefs is vital to a people fighting at the front. And the knowledge that your people are supporting you gives purpose and courage to armed forces of all kinds. Warriors are fed by affection as well as food.' (Slim, *Killing Civilians*, 195). He also notes, astutely, that 'the majority of politicians and commanders leading their nation or community into war desperately want to involve civilians in this way' (ibid. 204–5).

Broadly speaking, there are two ways to contribute to micro- and macro-threats. Either one is the agent of the threat or one contributes to a threat ultimately posed by someone else. Whether through fear, disgust, principle, lack of opportunity or ineptitude, many combatants are wholly ineffective in war, and make little or no contribution either to specific micro-threats or to the macro-threat posed by their side (some are a positive hindrance). The much-cited research of Brigadier-General S. L. A. Marshall claimed that only 15 to 25 per cent of Allied soldiers in the Second World War who could have fired their weapons did so.[26] Marshall's research methods have been criticized,[27] but others corroborate his basic findings, arguing that most soldiers have a natural aversion to killing, which even intensive psychological training may not overcome.[28] This is especially likely in the less professional armies against which liberal democracies tend to fight.[29]

Many other combatants play only a facilitating role, without directly contributing to specific micro-threats. Military units rely on cooks, medics, mechanics, and engineers, who support their more lethal comrades. These are especially numerous in the air force and the navy: for example, a Nimitz-class aircraft carrier has a crew of over 5,500, but houses only sixty to eighty aircraft and has around ten principal armaments. Only a very small proportion of the crew can be directly responsible for specific micro-threats.[30] Many of the rest facilitate those threats, and so make only small contributions to the overall macro-threat.

Other combatants neither pose nor contribute to immediate micro-threats, and also do little or nothing to advance the overall macro-threat. Consider, for example, reservists behind enemy lines, who have yet to arrive at the front; or a company that has finished its tour of duty and is being withdrawn; or an enemy barracks, when all

[26] S. L. A. Marshall, *Men Against Fire* (Gloucester: Peter Smith, 1978).

[27] Joanna Bourke, *An Intimate History of Killing* (London: Granta, 1999).

[28] David Grossman, *On Killing* (London: Back Bay Books, 1995); David Lee, *Up Close and Personal* (London: Greenhill, 2006); Mark Nicol, *Condor Blues* (Edinburgh: Mainstream, 2007).

[29] Grossman, *On Killing*.   [30] Thanks to Klem Ryan for suggesting this.

but those keeping watch are asleep. Consider also support staff who play an ostensibly restraining role, such as Judge Advocate Generals. Finally, all wars are morally heterogeneous, with just and unjust operations and phases. Unjust combatants might contribute to limited just goals, while just combatants might contribute to unjust ones.[31] In particular, individual acts of self- and other-defence by unjust combatants may often be permissible, for example when they are defending their own innocent compatriots against collateral or intentional harm.[32] And if you are responsible only for justified threats, then you cannot be liable to be killed.

Meanwhile, individual noncombatants also contribute in negligible, insignificant ways to micro- and macro-threats posed by their community. In modern industrialized countries as much as 25 per cent of the population works in war-related industries;[33] we provide the belligerents with crucial financial and other services; we support and sustain the soldiers who do the fighting; we pay our taxes and in democracies we vote, providing the economic and political resources without which war would be impossible. Our contributions to the state's capacity over time give it the strength and support to concentrate on war. We contribute, too, to the fighting capacities of specific combatants: for example, the maths teacher who imparts to a student the skills later necessary to his role as a gunner; the parent who brings up a strong, lethal son. Even children might make relevant contributions, by motivating their parents to fight.[34] Nor is this observation new. In the twelfth century, John of Salisbury argued that:

The hand of the commonwealth is either armed or unarmed. The armed hand...performs the soldiering of camps and blood; the unarmed...

---

[31] I give a detailed argument for how some unjust combatants can be justified in fighting in Lazar, 'Associative Duties'.

[32] On this point, see Uwe Steinhoff, 'Jeff McMahan on the Moral Inequality of Combatants', *Journal of Political Philosophy*, 16/2 (2008), 220–6.

[33] Downes, 'Desperate Times', 157–8. See also Gross, *Moral Dilemmas of Modern War*, 159; Slim, *Killing Civilians*: 189–91; Valentino et al., 'Bear Any Burden?', 351; Zohar, 'Collective War', 615.

[34] Zohar, 'Collective War'.

administers justice and, keeping holiday from arms, is enlisted in the service of the law. For not those alone do military service for the commonwealth who...ply their swords...against the foe, but also the advocates and pleaders of causes who...lift up the fallen, refresh the weary.[35]

If some negligible degree of individual responsibility for the threats posed by our state is what grounds liability, then few of us will be immune.

These general empirical considerations are persuasive, but perhaps not decisive. We can bolster them by appealing to some further a priori reasons in favour of the *Overlap Hypothesis*. First, imagine the extraordinary good fortune that would be involved were the *Overlap Hypothesis* false. Revisionists want the costs of war to track responsibility. It would be remarkable if the chaos and carnage of war could reflect such an ambitious principle of justice. What matters for liability is *individual* responsibility. But individuals are radically heterogeneous; we differ in innumerable respects. It would be very surprising if merely being a member of the armed forces were enough to ensure that one is more responsible for unjustified threats than any person who is not a combatant.

This sort of good fortune is highly unlikely. I find the following description of warfare, from Michael Herr's memoir of the Vietnam War, much more realistic:

At night in Khe Sanh, waiting there, thinking about all of them (40,000 some said), thinking that they might really try it, could keep you up. If they did, when they did, it might not matter that you were in the best bunker in the DMZ, wouldn't matter that you were young and had plans, that you were loved, that you were a non-combatant, an observer. Because if it came, it would be a bloodswarm of killing, and credentials would not be examined.[36]

Second, denying the *Overlap Hypothesis* implies an inadequate recognition of why warfare is so deeply problematic. If the harms inflicted in war could be apportioned to their victims' degree of responsibility, then

---

[35] In Reichberg et al., *Ethics of War*, 127.
[36] Michael Herr, *Dispatches* (London: Picador, 2004), 134.

fighting war would not be as morally troubling as it self-evidently is. Part of the tragedy of warfare is that, even when we have profoundly weighty reasons to fight, doing so inevitably involves so much morally objectionable killing. The *Overlap Hypothesis* explains why this is so; its denial asserts the possibility of a morally pure war, which any serious account of war's morality should view as a contradiction in terms. Killing in war is inherently chaotic and impersonal. Any theory of our right to life that is sufficiently undiscriminating to render this carnage rights-consistent is not discriminating enough to be an adequate theory of our right to life.

Third, conceding the truth of the *Overlap Hypothesis* is an important corollary of rejecting an unattractive picture of responsibility for warfare. In modern democratic states, our armed forces are our agents, subject to civilian control.[37] They fight at the behest of leaders whom we elect, and with resources that we provide. To deny that the civilian populations they serve bear any responsibility for their wars is either to doubt whether the armed forces are genuinely subject to democratic control or to outsource responsibility for the actions of our community. While none of us lives in perfect democracies, we cannot dissociate ourselves so thoroughly from the moral implications of our agents' actions. We have already shifted the physical burdens of our wars onto a subset of the population; we cannot defensibly shift the moral burdens as well.[38]

Finally, even those who still insist that combatants are consistently more responsible for unjustified threats than noncombatants in war should be moved by the following objection. As we have seen, they must determine where the threshold of responsibility for liability should fall. Suppose that we set the threshold very low, and say that when killing A is a necessary means to avert a sufficiently serious unjustified threat, if A is at all responsible for that threat coming about, then she can be liable to be killed. On this low-threshold view,

---

[37] Of course, in non-democratic states this is not true; equally, however, members of the armed forces of those states are often proportionately less responsible for their role therein.

[38] Cheyney Ryan, *The Chickenhawk Syndrome: War, Sacrifice, and Personal Responsibility* (London: Rowman & Littlefield, 2009).

few people in a modern state will escape liability—as already noted, most of us, even children, contribute, however marginally and insubstantially, to our government's capacity to wage wars. Clearly this is too little responsibility to ground liability to be killed.

But the only explanation of this judgement is that we think there should be some degree of 'fit' between what the target has done and the fate of losing her right to life. This judgement reflects an implicit commitment to a high non-comparative threshold, below which one is simply not responsible enough to be liable to be killed. But if there has to be a fit between what you have done and your becoming liable to be killed, then how can we assert that all the combatants whom we will intentionally kill in war are liable? They are unified only by their combatant status. Their responsibility for unjustified threats will vary widely. It should be a truism about war that this fit does not obtain for many of them. To render all the combatants whom we will intentionally kill liable to be killed, we need to deny the need for a fit between degree of responsibility and the fate of losing one's right to life; but if we deny that fit, then we cannot deny that many noncombatants will also be liable to be killed in war.

Competing speculations about the *Overlap Hypothesis* will never be decisive. But the general empirical case seems sound, and these a priori arguments give further support. In the rest of this book, I will steer clear of wishful thinking and presuppose that the Hypothesis is true. Even in the 'best' wars, a morally significant proportion of enemy soldiers and civilians will be responsible to just the same degree for contributing to unjustified threats. If we are to defend *Moral Distinction*, therefore, we cannot rely on responsibility alone.

However, the arguments that follow do not depend on endorsing my broader view of the morality of war, or even on endorsing the *Overlap Hypothesis*. Even if you think that (amazingly) we can fight wars in which all and only unjust combatants are liable to be killed, *Moral Distinction* is still a highly plausible principle, and your theory is strengthened if you can explain it.[39] If the invasion of Iraq in 2003

---

[39] Some philosophers now argue that liability and lesser-evil justifications can subsist alongside one another, so that even if a given unjust combatant is not liable

was unjust, then each Iraqi combat death was wrongful. But killing the thousands of civilians who died in that invasion was still worse. All killing in the pursuit of unjust aims is wrong. But some such killings are clearly worse than others.[40] Vindicating this judgement enhances any account of the morality of war; failing to do so is a serious theoretical cost.

5. Arguing for *Moral Distinction*

Everyone needs an argument for *Moral Distinction*. The best defence of this principle will rest on multiple overlapping foundations— properties that consistently but contingently co-vary with noncombatant status. Each of these properties makes killing civilians worse than killing soldiers. Each will have exceptions, but taken together they will robustly protect civilians in war. And if a civilian or soldier is an exception to each of the overlapping foundations, then she is a legitimate exception to the principle. In other words, it is not combatant or noncombatant status that explains *Moral Distinction*, but rather these other morally relevant properties. In this book, I focus on the core arguments explaining why killing civilians is worse than killing soldiers. Examining in detail the fuzzy line between these

to be killed, as long as he is liable to *some* harm, the additional harm beyond what he is liable to can be justified as a lesser evil. Whatever the merits of this mixed-justification view, note that the same dilemma arises here as before. Many noncombatants will be responsible to just the same degree as many combatants, so like those combatants will be liable to some harm, if not liable to be killed. So, if a mixed justification makes it permissible to kill those combatants, it will do the same for those noncombatants. This means that we still need *Moral Distinction* both to justify killing combatants in war and to rule out killing noncombatants. See Jeff McMahan, 'Who is Morally Liable to be Killed in War?', *Analysis*, 71/3 (2011), 544–59; Jeff McMahan, 'What Rights may be Defended by Means of War?', in Seth Lazar and Cécile Fabre (eds), *The Morality of Defensive War* (Oxford: OUP, 2014), 115–58; Saba Bazargan, 'Killing Minimally Responsible Threats', *Ethics*, 125/1 (2014), 114–36.

[40] As one reflection of how widespread this judgement is, note how easy it is to find sources on how many civilians died in the Iraq invasion (estimates vary from around 3,500 to around 7,500), and how hard to find statistics on the number of combatant deaths. See <www.comw.org/pda/0310rm8.html>, <http://costsofwar.org/sites/default/files/articles/15/attachments/Iraqciv2013.pdf>, <https://www.iraqbodycount.org>.

classes is beyond my remit. But we can arbitrate hard cases by considering whether and how these properties apply.

Although responsibility and liability cannot alone explain the ethics of killing in war, they are nonetheless essential. Any defence of *Moral Distinction* must start with liability, since this is the most important determinant of permissible killing in war. I think the best approach is to start with a high threshold, grounded in the non-comparative view of liability. On this view, almost all noncombatants are innocent in war. The negligible, unnecessary, marginal contributions that they make to the threats posed by their community are not substantial enough to make them liable to be killed. The necessary fit between their behaviour and that fate is missing. I will not argue at length for this threshold, though my considered judgement on this is as firm as any such judgement I can make, and certainly firmer than my intuitions about any of the elaborate hypothetical cases usually invoked to challenge this view. Indeed, I think a test of the plausibility of a theory of liability is whether it leaves ordinary civilians liable to be killed in war. If it does, then it had better have some serious theoretical virtues to overcome that counterintuitive result. That said, some of the arguments to follow would work for a low threshold as well.

Of course, even on a high-threshold view, some civilians can be liable. Political leaders, some financiers, media moguls, and other such figures of influence might be liable to be killed in virtue of influencing others to fight unjust wars. But almost all ordinary non-combatants are innocent. This is the first step on the path to *Moral Distinction*, but it is also a crucial premise in the arguments for noncombatant immunity, proportionality, and precautions in attack. Those principles presuppose not only that killing civilians is worse than killing soldiers, but that killing civilians is very bad indeed. We need both the relative and the absolute claim to get those constraints off the ground.

If so many noncombatants are innocent, then many combatants will be innocent too. Few on the just side will be liable, but many unjust combatants will also be innocent. The argument for *Moral*

Distinction, then, is disjunctive: killing civilians is worse than killing soldiers, either because the soldiers are liable and the civilians are not, or because killing innocent civilians is worse than killing innocent soldiers. My focus in this book is on the second disjunct.

6. Prospectus

In the remaining chapters of this book, I canvass five arguments for *Moral Distinction*. I begin by considering an instrumental case, according to which killing civilians is worse than killing soldiers, just because it is so ineffective that it cannot satisfy a necessity constraint on permissible killing.[41] No doubt killing civilians is often wanton and pointless, which partly explains why it is so egregiously wrong. But this alone is not enough. Instrumental reasons are least effective when civilians are most vulnerable—when belligerents reasonably believe that harming civilians *does* minimize wrongful suffering, because it is necessary to achieve their aims.[42] This is when civilians need *Moral Distinction* most, but instrumental arguments protect them least. Moreover, even if this instrumental argument could overcome these objections, it would vindicate *Moral Distinction* for the wrong reasons. The outrage we feel when villages are burned, hospitals gutted, and schools bombed is not pragmatically motivated.

---

[41] George I. Mavrodes, 'Conventions and the Morality of War', *Philosophy and Public Affairs*, 4/2 (1975), 117–31; Janina Dill and Henry Shue, 'Limiting the Killing in War: Military Necessity and the St. Petersburg Assumption', *Ethics and International Affairs*, 26/3 (2012), 311–33.

[42] For chilling historical research to support this point, see Benjamin A. Valentino, *Final Solutions: Mass Killing and Genocide in the Twentieth Century* (Ithaca, NY: Cornell University Press, 2004). For more recent examples, see the public justifications offered for the apparently disproportionate harms inflicted on Gazan civilians in the 2014 Gaza War, which appealed to their military necessity: Herb Keinon, 'PM: Terrorists Watching whether World Gives Immunity for Attacks from Schools, Homes', *Jerusalem Post*, 6 Aug. 2014, <www.jpost.com/Operation-Protective-Edge/WATCH-LIVE-Netanyahu-addresses-foreign-press-in-aftermath-of-Gaza-operation-370255>; Yishai Schwartz, 'Israel's Deadly Invasion of Gaza is Morally Justified', *New Republic*, 21 July 2014, <www.newrepublic.com/article/118788/israels-war-gaza-morally-justified>.

The remaining chapters concentrate on non-instrumental arguments for *Moral Distinction*. Chapter 3 asks whether killing civilians in war makes use of them in an especially wrongful way, whereas killing soldiers involves a less objectionable form of harmful agency. Certainly, attacks on noncombatants are often *opportunistically* intended: twentieth-century strategic bombing, for example, was explicitly conceived as a means to 'break the will' of the adversary, either coercing its leaders to surrender or causing the polity to rise up and overthrow them.[43] Attacks on combatants, by contrast, are often *eliminative*: the defender gains nothing by killing them that he would not have enjoyed in their absence. If opportunistic killings are worse than eliminative ones, then killing civilians is worse than killing soldiers.

In Chapter 4 I turn to risk. I first argue that riskier killings are, other things equal, worse than less risky killings. I then argue that, because civilians are more likely to be innocent than are soldiers, with rare exceptions, killing civilians is riskier than killing soldiers. So, I conclude, killing civilians is worse than killing soldiers.

Chapter 5 explores the moral significance of vulnerability and defencelessness. I first analyse these much-used but undertheorized concepts, then present several arguments to show that killing the vulnerable and defenceless is, other things equal, worse than killing those who are less vulnerable and defenceless. I then show that civilians are more vulnerable and defenceless than are soldiers.

All the arguments so far focus on showing that killing civilians is worse than killing soldiers. In Chapter 6, I shift focus, and argue that killing soldiers is better than killing civilians. In other words, I argue for 'combatant non-immunity', focusing on combatants' recklessness, their willingness to draw fire away from their civilian population, arguments from complicity and positive duties, on the legal standing of killing in war, and on combatants' voluntary exposure of themselves to risk.

---

[43] Giulio Douhet, *The Command of the Air* (Washington, DC: Office of Air Force History, 1983).

Each of the arguments presented in Chapters 2–6 contributes to the justification of *Moral Distinction*. Each is subject to exceptions. Only when all are considered in concert do we have grounds for this principle that are as robust as its intuitive support.

In the Battle of the Bzura, September 1939, the German 10th Army crushed several infantry divisions of the Polish Army. The Wehrmacht killed perhaps 20,000 Polish soldiers. At the same time, Nazi forces were carrying out Operation Tannenberg, slaughtering 20,000 Polish civilians over two months, shot and buried in mass graves. No doubt, the invading army wrongly killed those Polish soldiers. But killing those civilians was still worse.

In Syria and Northern Iraq, in 2014, the Islamic State was locked in battle with the Peshmerga. If ever there was a just cause, it was defending Kurdistan against the predations of these Manichaean militants. Almost certainly, every Peshmerga guerrilla killed by Islamic State was killed wrongfully. But still, IS attacks on Yazidi civilians were worse.

These judgements reflect the common-sense morality of war, and *Moral Distinction* is at its heart. Until recently, it stood at the centre of just war theory too. But recent work has undermined familiar arguments in *Moral Distinction*'s favour. It has suggested that the real dividing line is between the just and the unjust, the responsible and the non-responsible. And that division does not respect the line between combatants and noncombatants.

At the same time, more and less scrupulous militants, politicians, and public intellectuals have espoused similar views in public debates over the ethics of force. They say that civilians' responsibility for the actions of their elected officials deprives them of their privileged status, leaving them no different from combatants.[44] They say that

---

[44] See e.g. Osama bin Laden's 'Letter to America', and the equally poisonous online editorial of retired Major-General Giora Eiland (a former Chief of the Israeli National Security Council). Osama Bin Laden, 'Letter to America', *Guardian*, <www.theguardian.com/world/2002/nov/24/theobserver>; Giora Eiland, 'In Gaza, there is No Such Thing as "Innocent Civilians"', *Ynetnews.com* (2014), <www.ynetnews.com/articles/0,7340,L-4554583,00.html>. Still more disturbing—because of the publication

the potential that any civilian will be conscripted makes them all legitimate targets.[45] They say that we must abandon restraint or else unjust foes will take advantage of our reserve.[46] They say that anyone killed by a drone attack counts as a combatant, just in case he is male, and of military age.[47]

Almost everyone agrees that killing civilians is worse than killing soldiers. But the voices of dissent are getting louder. No principle is more fundamental to the ethics of war than this one. We should mobilize all the resources of moral and political philosophy in its defence.

---

venue, and the audience reached—is a similar argument made by Thane Rosenbaum in the Wall Street Journal: Thane Rosenbaum, 'Hamas's Civilian Death Strategy', *Wall Street Journal* (2014), <www.wsj.com/articles/thane-rosenbaum-civilian-casualties-in-gaza-1405970362>. It was syndicated to (at least) *The Australian* and *Jerusalem Post*.

[45] As discussed (with a quote from Sheikh Ahmed Yassin, one of the founders of Hamas) in this Human Rights Watch report: *Erased in a Moment: Suicide Bombing Attacks against Israeli Civilians* (New York: Human Rights Watch, 2002). See <www.hrw.org/reports/2002/isrl-pa/ISRAELPA1002-04.htm#P678_150385>.

[46] Schwartz, 'Israel's Deadly Invasion'; Keinon, 'Terrorists Watching'.

[47] Scott Shane and Jo Becker, 'Secret "Kill List" Proves a Test of Obama's Principles and Will', *New York Times*, <www.nytimes.com/2012/05/29/world/obamas-leadership-in-war-on-al-qaeda.html?smid=pl-share>.

2

Necessity

1. Introduction

On 9 August 1945, the bombardier of *Bockscar*, a United States Air Force B29, dropped Fat Man, an atomic bomb with a core of 6.4kg of plutonium, on Nagasaki. Even though the hills around the Urakami Valley disrupted the blast, it killed as many as 80,000 people.

Early that morning, in accordance with the Yalta agreement, the Soviets had invaded the Japanese puppet state of Manchukuo. Days before, Fat Man's little brother had killed 140,000 people in Hiroshima. The Japanese leadership was in turmoil.

Perhaps political scientist Robert Pape is right, and neither bomb played a significant role in the Japanese decision to surrender, on 15 August.[1] But even if he is wrong about that, surely bombing Nagasaki was unnecessary. The Japanese had been in retreat for two years. The Red Army had a clear advantage in Manchukuo; the first bomb had established US aerial dominance; the Allies had captured Iwo Jima and Okinawa, and were preparing for an invasion. Even if some victims of the bomb were munitions workers, who might be thought responsible for contributing to the threats posed by their state, many thousands were just ordinary people, trying to survive the war. They were killed pointlessly.

Killing civilians is often pointless. It achieves nothing, beyond the suffering that it inflicts. Killing soldiers is often crucial to achieving

[1] Robert Pape, *Bombing to Win: Air Power and Coercion in War* (London: Cornell University Press, 1996).

victory. We might then argue from necessity to *Moral Distinction*: unnecessary killing is worse than necessary killing; so killing civilians is worse than killing soldiers, because killing soldiers is necessary, killing civilians is not.

This basic insight is used in very different accounts of the morality of war. If killing civilians is not necessary to win wars, then the rule that protects them can be agreed to by all belligerents without diminishing their chances of success. And since it reduces the scope and scale of suffering in wartime, it is in their interests to agree. So we have a contractarian justification for the protection of civilians in war.[2] A rule-consequentialist could reach the same conclusion more directly: if killing civilians serves little purpose, protecting them is a relatively cost-free way to reduce the suffering caused by war.[3] From the same empirical premise, rights-based approaches can deliver the same result: killing even apparently liable civilians is impermissible if it is unnecessary. Even if a low degree of responsibility is sufficient for liability, and many noncombatants are potentially liable to be killed, killing liable civilians is worse than killing liable soldiers, because killing the civilians (but not the soldiers) is unnecessary.[4] Likewise on a high-threshold view: killing innocent civilians unnecessarily is surely

[2]   Yitzhak Benbaji, 'The Moral Power of Soldiers to Undertake the Duty of Obedience', *Ethics*, 122/1 (2011), 43–73.

[3]   Judith Lichtenberg, 'War, Innocence, and the Doctrine of Double Effect', *Philosophical Studies*, 74/3 (1994), 366; George I. Mavrodes, 'Conventions and the Morality of War', *Philosophy and Public Affairs*, 4/2 (1975), 125; Henry Shue, 'Targeting Civilian Infrastructure with Smart Bombs: The New Permissiveness', *Philosophy and Public Policy Quarterly*, 30/3 (2010), 3.

[4]   Richard J. Arneson, 'Just Warfare Theory and Noncombatant Immunity', *Cornell International Law Journal*, 39 (2006), 663–88; Cécile Fabre, 'Guns, Food, and Liability to Attack in War', *Ethics*, 120/1 (2009), 63; Helen Frowe, 'Self-Defence and the Principle of Non-Combatant Immunity', *Journal of Moral Philosophy*, (2011), 19–20; Michael Gross, 'Killing Civilians Intentionally: Double Effect, Reprisal, and Necessity in the Middle East', *Political Science Quarterly*, 120/4 (2005–6), 566; Jeff McMahan, *Killing in War* (Oxford: OUP, 2009), 225; Lionel McPherson, 'Innocence and Responsibility in War', *Canadian Journal of Philosophy*, 34/4 (2004), 505; Gerhard Øverland, 'Killing Civilians', *European Journal of Philosophy*, 13/3 (2005), 352, 360; Judith Jarvis Thomson, 'Self-Defense', *Philosophy and Public Affairs*, 20/4 (1991), 297. Note that on McMahan's view, if killing someone is unnecessary to achieve one's goals, then they are not in fact liable to be killed.

worse than killing innocent combatants when it is necessary to achieving some good end.

The Necessity Argument is promising: what could be more obvious than that killing people pointlessly is wrong? It is also politic. It is much easier to advocate adherence to a norm that is in everyone's interests: if the argument is right, then the protection of civilians in war is costless. Necessity is also undoubtedly one important foundation of *Moral Distinction*. Killing civilians is often so absolutely bad, and so much worse than killing soldiers, because it is wanton and pointless. But necessity cuts both ways: though it can constrain, sometimes it permits. And it threatens to protect noncombatants least when they need it most. It is part of the story, but we cannot rest here. Or so I will now argue.

2. How do we Test for Necessity in War?

Although philosophers and public figures often allude to the argument from necessity when advocating *Moral Distinction*, surprisingly few have expanded on its normative or its empirical premises. This section presents a working analysis of necessity and a methodology for testing the argument's empirical claim.

The first step is to clear up some confusing terminology. In international law and military discourse, military necessity is typically understood as simply meaning military advantage.[5] On this view, anything that increases the likelihood and reduces the costs of victory is considered militarily necessary. Obviously it is not this understanding of necessity in war that grounds the Necessity Argument.

The argument depends instead on a more general normative principle, which is indeed frequently recognized in international law and

---

[5] 'Military necessity permits a belligerent, subject to the laws of war, to apply any amount and kind of force to compel the complete submission of the enemy with the least possible expenditure of time, life, and money': USA v. List et al. (American Military Tribunal, Nuremberg, 1948), 11 NMT 1230, 1253. See also the definition of necessity in US Army, 'Civilian Casualty Mitigation', *Army Tactics, Techniques and Procedures*, 3-37.31 (2012), 1–8.

military discourse: inflicting unnecessary suffering is always wrong. Undeserved, involuntary human suffering is always a bad thing, and is *pro tanto* proscribed. If it is unnecessary, then nothing overrides this *pro tanto* prohibition. For a harmful course of action to qualify as necessary, it must satisfy all of three conditions:

1. The harmful course of action must advance a goal. It must be neither wholly wanton, nor an end in itself. Harm that contributes nothing to achieving an objective is inescapably unnecessary.

2. No less harmful course of action has equal or better prospects of achieving the goal. If the agent could have as good a prospect of bringing about the goal while inflicting less harm, then the additional harm done serves no purpose, and so is unnecessary.

3. If there is a less harmful course of action that could achieve the goal, but is less likely to succeed, then the difference in prospects of success—or effectiveness—must be enough to justify the difference in harm inflicted. Suppose that, if the agent inflicts H harm, he has a 0.8 probability of achieving the goal, but if he inflicts H/2 harm, he has a 0.3 probability of success. The less harmful option involves the agent absorbing a 0.5 reduction in his probability of success. The more harmful option satisfies necessity only if avoiding this cost to the agent justifies the additional harm inflicted on the victim.

The normative premise of the Necessity Argument is uncontroversial. Harm is always a bad thing. Inflicting undeserved, involuntary harm without achieving any corresponding good is always wrong (whether one's target is liable or innocent). So, if killing civilians in war does not satisfy these three conditions, while killing soldiers does, then killing civilians is worse than killing soldiers, and we have a solid argument for *Moral Distinction*.

Before thinking about how to test the argument's empirical premise, however, we should note two very obvious limitations of arguing for *Moral Distinction* in this way. First, killing civilians is clearly sometimes necessary, when we cannot achieve a vital military objective except through action that will unavoidably kill some civilians.

Foreseen but unintended ('collateral') killing of civilians often satisfies all three conditions for necessity. So the Necessity Argument cannot explain why collaterally killing civilians is worse than killing soldiers. Some think that collateral killing cannot, by definition, be necessary, since harm is necessary only if it is a means to an end, and collateral killings cannot be means. This is a mistake. Suppose I can capture a building without killing any bystanders, by clearing it on foot, but I nonetheless choose to call in artillery fire and destroy it, knowing that many civilians will be killed. I did not intend the civilians' deaths, but they were clearly unnecessary, and this is part of what makes them so objectionable.

Second, killing satisfies necessity only if it is an unavoidable element of a course of action that achieves some correspondingly weighty good. But if harm is inflicted in pursuit of an unjustified goal, then there is no good to outweigh the bad of harming. Suppose a thief cannot steal diamonds from a jewellery store without killing the security guard. In a morally neutral sense, killing the guard is necessary to achieve the thief's ends. But in the morally rich sense of necessity, it is clearly *not* necessary, since the thief achieves nothing that could counterbalance taking the guard's life. The Necessity Argument cannot differentiate between killing civilians and soldiers when the ends aimed at are bad ones.

These limitations should not be overstated. If much of the collateral killing of civilians were unnecessary, while much of the collateral killing of combatants were necessary, then we should still think killing civilians worse than killing soldiers. Conversely, if we rely on the Necessity Argument to protect civilians in war, then the scope for collateral killing of noncombatants will significantly increase. And I will argue in Chapter 4 that if you believe you are pursuing a justified goal, and if it is unlikely that killing this person will be necessary to achieve it, then killing him is objectively worse than killing someone whose death is more likely to be necessary. So, a cousin of the Necessity Argument applies when the ends aimed at are merely believed to be justified.

Still, the Necessity Argument cannot provide a fully general argument for protecting civilians in war. It can at best be one of the multiple overlapping foundations of *Moral Distinction*.

To test the argument's empirical premise, we need first to identify the tactics whose necessity we shall investigate. I will focus on *civilian victimization*, which includes both intentional killing of civilians and intuitively excessive collateral killing. I will also call these 'anti-civilian tactics'. If intentionally killing civilians is sometimes necessary, then that is a significant count against the Necessity Argument. I will not try to define what counts as excessive collateral killing, but I will show that the Necessity Argument licenses an overly permissive stance on killing civilians as a side-effect.

Working out whether civilian victimization satisfies the three conditions for necessity in war is difficult. How do we tell whether a tactic is effective? Obviously, experimental verification is out of the question, so we can only interpret the historical record. But where strategic success follows civilian victimization, how can we know how crucial those tactics were to bringing about that success? After defeat, should we blame the anti-civilian tactics or might defeat have resulted solely from other factors?[6]

The confusion endemic to conflict exacerbates these familiar problems. They are further aggravated if we adopt the moralized understanding of necessity, which requires us to know whether each operation achieved something morally worthwhile. For each case, we would have to determine not only whether the belligerent's war was just as a whole, but also whether this particular attack was justified. Both of these matters will be controversial—indeed, merely working out the correct principles would be hard enough. Not only would this make the Necessity Argument contingent on resolving moral questions that are each as complex and controversial as those

---

[6] Colin S. Gray, *Modern Strategy* (Oxford: OUP, 1999), 295–6; Matthew Adam Kocher et al., 'Aerial Bombing and Counterinsurgency in the Vietnam War', *American Journal of Political Science*, 55/2 (2011), 2; Robert Pape, 'The Strategic Logic of Suicide Terrorism', *American Political Science Review*, 97/3 (2003), 351.

around *Moral Distinction*, it would also radically reduce the dataset from which inferences could be drawn.

However, we can overcome these worries if the intermediate objectives of just and unjust conflicts (and those that fall in between) are the same. Provided a belligerent is aiming at a *kind* of goal that a just belligerent could aim at, then if a tactic has been necessary (in the morally neutral sense) to achieve that goal, we can infer that it could also be necessary (in the morally rich sense) to achieving a just one.

Imagine (not implausibly) that only unjust wars had ever been fought, but that we now have to fight a just war. Suppose you, the commander-in-chief, ask your generals to plan an operation that satisfies necessity. They could surely draw lessons from the history of warfare, from scenarios that were sufficiently similar to their own except that the relevant belligerent had unjust goals. What was necessary in the neutral sense for their antecedents could be necessary in the rich sense for them. The mere fact that the dataset differs in this way from their own experience cannot block the inference from one set of cases to the other.

Of course, sometimes specific reasons block that inference. If a historical belligerent's objective could not possibly be aimed at by a just belligerent, then the necessity of victimizing civilians to achieve that objective is irrelevant to necessity in just wars. This is most obvious when the belligerent specifically aims to harm civilians. If the goal is genocide or ethnic cleansing, civilian victimization will clearly be necessary in the neutral sense, but since just belligerents obviously could not aim at these objectives, this is irrelevant to the Necessity Argument.

If our dataset includes only cases in which the objectives *could* be aimed at by a just belligerent, then we can infer from the historical record conclusions about necessity in just wars. Just belligerents can fight interstate conflicts over disputed territory, rebellions against oppressive incumbents, and counterinsurgencies against unjust rebellions. So if civilian victimization is necessary in historical conflicts like these, it can be necessary in just wars too, irrespective of whether the historical conflicts were themselves just.

Many of the historical examples discussed in this chapter were obviously unjust. But for each of them, there is a counterfactual scenario in which a belligerent pursues the same kind of objective justifiably. If a future belligerent encounters a situation like that faced by some historical belligerent—one sufficiently similar in all morally relevant respects except that the future belligerent's goals are justified, while its historical counterpart's goals were not—then if it was necessary in the neutral sense for the historical belligerent to use some tactic, we can reasonably infer that this tactic could be necessary in the morally rich sense for the future belligerent. If, in the past, an insurgent group fighting an unjust rebellion has found strategic success through anti-civilian tactics when no other options were available, then we can infer that in a future just rebellion anti-civilian tactics might again be the only viable option left, and so satisfy morally rich necessity.

To satisfy the first condition of necessity, civilian victimization must advance goals that a just belligerent could aim at. Showing this is challenging enough; evaluating whether the second and third conditions for necessity are satisfied would add further serious difficulties. We would have to compare the chosen tactics with untaken options, counterfactuals about which we can only speculate. By narrowing our research question, we can keep a tighter grip on that speculation.[7] Our question is: have tactics involving civilian victimization

---

[7] Jeff McMahan has raised the following challenge to the examples on which this discussion draws. He notes that the effectiveness of anti-civilian tactics 'depends to a very considerable extent on the nature of the regime against which it is used', in particular, on the target being a liberal democracy, since dictators are unlikely to care about harm to noncombatant citizens (McMahan, personal communication on file). He then notes that just wars are often fought by liberal democracies against tyrannical or authoritarian regimes, and anti-civilian tactics are likely to be less effective. This means that what we really need are data on the rate of success for anti-civilian tactics used by liberal democracies fighting just wars against non-democratic states. Some research has been done on related topics—the broad consensus is that democracies are more likely to make concessions to terrorism than non-democracies (although there is strong dissent from Max Abrahms: see below); and Alexander Downes has shown that, whatever their success rates, liberal democracies are no less likely to use anti-civilian tactics than other polities: Alexander Downes, 'Restraint or Propellant? Democracy and Civilian Fatalities in Interstate Wars', *Journal of Conflict Resolution*,

ever achieved objectives that a just belligerent could aim at, when no other effective option was available? Denying that such cases can arise is necessary, though not sufficient, to justify the Necessity Argument; a strong argument that they do arise would weaken it.[8]

3. The Case Against Civilian Victimization

Showing that civilian victimization is never effective is harder than showing it sometimes works. And yet, if it fails in a wide range of conflicts, then that would support the Necessity Argument. In this section I discuss research that supports this response, looking at aerial bombing in interstate conflict, at counterinsurgency, and at terrorism.

In *Bombing to Win* (1996) Robert Pape famously argued that aerial bombing of civilians is strategically redundant. Distinguishing between punishment and denial tactics—the former inflict civilian suffering to coerce concessions (either directly or through popular uprising); the latter neutralize the adversary's military capacities, from production, through supply line to battlefield—he argues that in forty campaigns between 1917 and 1991, punishment bombing has not worked.[9]

Pape's principal target, besides late twentieth-century US strategic doctrine, is Giulio Douhet, whose 1921 book *Command of the Air* is the *locus classicus* of punishment-based aerial bombing in

51/6 (2007), 872–904. I think, however, that to focus only on just wars is problematic, owing to the great difficulties in determining whether a given war is just. Additionally, although anti-civilian tactics may typically prove ineffective against authoritarian regimes, liberal democracies fighting just wars might well face other adversaries. Moreover, liberal democracies may face insurgencies, against which anti-civilian tactics can be effective, not only as a coercive tool, but as a means of preventing civilians from helping the insurgents.

[8] This also allows reference to existing research on the strategic success of civilian victimization. If just war theorists are to test their theories against the empirical record while remaining philosophers, then they had better be able to make use of the research by political scientists and international relations scholars who address these problems empirically.

[9] Pape, *Bombing to Win.*

strategic theory. In the Second World War, British Bomber Command explicitly endorsed the Douhet approach: the bombing of Germany left 7.5 million people homeless; 305,000 civilians were killed; 780,000 wounded. Cologne, Hamburg, and Dresden were flattened, in the hope of prompting the people to rise up and stop the war.[10]

And yet Pape argues that the anti-civilian bombing of Germany contributed little to Allied victory. It neither compelled the Nazi regime to make concessions, nor prompted an uprising against it. Similarly, Japanese government records suggest that anti-civilian tactics there were largely irrelevant to their surrender, which was determined more by the advancing Soviet Army than by worries about civilians. Pape analyses three other cases that might be thought counterexamples (Korea, Vietnam, Iraq 1991: all bombed by the US), and argues that in none did punishment bombing contribute to victory.[11] Bombing civilians, he concludes, has never caused uprisings against the adversary regime.[12]

Why does Douhet bombing fail? Pape notes that in Germany nationalist sentiment, government propaganda, and state repression stopped civilian victimization leading to anti-war protests.[13] Additionally, terrible attacks on civilians leave them primarily concerned with survival, rather than with bigger political issues; indeed, they make civilians more loyal, since only their government can offer protection.[14] More generally, Pape argues that nation-states can tolerate high costs for their vital interests and national pride. They can also mitigate the bad effects of punishment bombing—perhaps not to the civilians' benefit, but enough at least to sustain their fighting capacity.[15]

---

[10] Pape, *Bombing to Win*, 271.   [11] Pape, *Bombing to Win*, 315.

[12] Pape, *Bombing to Win*, 271–2. See also Michael Horowitz and Dan Reiter, 'When does Aerial Bombing Work? Quantitative Empirical Tests, 1917–1999', *Journal of Conflict Resolution*, 45/2 (2001), 147–73.

[13] Pape, *Bombing to Win*, 271–2.   [14] Pape, *Bombing to Win*, 271–2.

[15] Pape, *Bombing to Win*, 316.

Some researchers of counterinsurgency have reached similar conclusions about the effectiveness of anti-civilian tactics, identifying three objections to indiscriminate civilian victimization. First, counterinsurgents need the support of those whom the insurgents claim to represent. The US *Counterinsurgency Field Manual* notes that 'counterinsurgents that use excessive force to limit short-term risk alienate the local populace. They deprive themselves of the support or tolerance of the people. This situation is what insurgents want. It increases the threat they pose.'[16] Insurgents intend their adversaries to overreact, because that strengthens their position. Excessive force generates anger, which triggers high-risk behaviour like joining the insurgency.[17]

The second argument extends the first: the domestic population is not the only relevant audience; often, the international community is watching too. If the counterinsurgent is internationally regarded as illegitimate that raises new obstacles to success. When counterinsurgents engage in civilian victimization, international disapprobation, economic sanctions, even foreign military intervention might ensue—witness Libya and Syria.

The third objection is more abstract. Counterinsurgents use force against civilians to compel compliance. But indiscriminate force is a blunt tool: if those who comply and those who refuse are equally likely to be killed, then why comply?[18] To work, coercive sanctions must be prompt, focused, proportionate, and consistent. Indiscriminate attacks on civilians meet none of these criteria.[19] Far from

---

[16] US Army, *Counterinsurgency Field Manual* (Washington, DC: US Army and US Marine Corps, 2006), §§7–24. This is also a consistent theme of US Army, 'Civilian Casualty Mitigation'.

[17] Stathis N. Kalyvas, 'The Paradox of Terrorism in Civil War', *Journal of Ethics*, 8/1 (2004), 116.

[18] Alexander Downes, 'Draining the Sea by Filling the Graves: Investigating the Effectiveness of Indiscriminate Violence as a Counterinsurgency Strategy', *Civil Wars*, 9/4 (2007), 426; Kalyvas, 'Paradox of Terrorism', 104; David Mason, 'Insurgency, Counterinsurgency, and the Rational Peasant', *Public Choice*, 86/1/2 (1996), 80.

[19] Kalyvas, 'Paradox of Terrorism', 118.

compelling compliance, they force civilians into the insurgents' arms, looking for protection.[20]

In counterinsurgency, scepticism about the efficacy of civilian victimization is common. In research on terrorism, the reverse view is more popular.[21] Those arguments are discussed later; here I focus on a prominent critique of this consensus.[22] It begins with a methodological objection: much of the research on terrorism's effectiveness 'rests on game-theoretic models, single case studies, or a handful of well-known terrorist victories', rather than broader empirical foundations.[23] In response, Max Abrahms examines twenty-eight groups classed by the US State Department as Foreign Terrorist Organizations before 2001, assessing their methods and their success rate. He identifies forty-two policy goals for the twenty-eight groups, and concludes that only three were either partially or fully achieved.[24] He notes, further, that groups that primarily target civilians achieve even limited successes only very rarely (again, he finds three examples).[25] He reasons that terrorists are more likely to succeed when they have limited territorial goals, but targeting civilians

---

[20] Jason Lyall, 'Does Indiscriminate Violence Incite Insurgent Attacks? Evidence from Chechnya', *Journal of Conflict Resolution*, 53/3 (2009), 335. See also Reed M. Wood, 'Rebel Capability and Strategic Violence against Civilians', *Journal of Peace Research*, 47/5 (2010), 603.

[21] Max Abrahms, 'Why Terrorism Does Not Work', *International Security*, 31/2 (2006), 44–5.

[22] Abrahms, 'Why Terrorism Does Not Work'; Max Abrahms, 'Why Democracies Make Superior Counterterrorists', *Security Studies*, 16/2 (2007), 223–53; William Rose, Rysla Murphy, and Max Abrahms, 'Does Terrorism Ever Work? The 2004 Madrid Train Bombings', *International Security*, 32/1 (2007), 185–92; Max Abrahms, 'What Terrorists Really Want: Terrorist Motives and Counterterrorism Strategy', *International Security*, 32/4 (2008), 78–105.

[23] Abrahms, 'Why Terrorism Does Not Work', 43.

[24] Hezbollah's expulsion of Israel from Southern Lebanon in 1984 and again in 2000 are coded as total successes, as is the Tamil Tigers' establishment of autonomy in Sri Lanka (the article was written in 2006). Abrahms aimed to be generous, e.g. counting both partial and total successes as policy successes, and only complete failure as failure, and attributing all successes to terrorism rather than to any other intervening variables: Abrahms, 'Why Terrorism Does Not Work', 51.

[25] The drawdown of US troops in Saudi Arabia post-9/11 is coded as a limited success, as is Israel's withdrawal from the Gaza Strip.

miscommunicates your policy objectives, suggesting that your aims are maximalist and ideological.[26] By killing civilians, terrorists engage the adversary's vital interests, and so invoke the same resilience and resistance that makes Douhet-style bombing so ineffective.[27]

4. Civilian Victimization Can Be Effective...

Notwithstanding the arguments of the previous section, other evidence suggests that civilian victimization can be effective in terrorism, counterinsurgency, and interstate conflict. The contrary conclusion misses the point that, when civilian victimization is ineffective, this is in part because it is already believed unjustified. It is also based on overly restrictive conceptualizations of the relevant anti-civilian tactics and how to measure their effectiveness. In this section I expand on these observations in turn, before noting how sometimes, even by the criteria set out above, civilian victimization appears to be effective.

First, each of Abrahms's, Kalyvas's, and Pape's arguments depends in part on how adversaries and bystanders respond to anti-civilian tactics. Pape stresses the resilience of nation-states, which rally around the flag when indiscriminately targeted; Kalyvas and the *Field Manual* argue that civilian victimization delegitimizes counterinsurgents among both domestic and international audiences; Abrahms emphasizes the role that responses play in rendering civilian victimization ineffective. These responses partly depend on the prior belief that attacks on civilians are unjustified. Otherwise attacking civilians would not delegitimize or elicit the same stoicism.

Second, Kalyvas, Abrahms, and Pape have too narrow an understanding of civilian victimization for their research to afford compelling support to the Necessity Argument (though that understanding was undoubtedly appropriate for their own research objectives). Each focuses on the efficacy of intentional, indiscriminate attacks on civilians, but this is not the only relevant form of civilian victimization. As

---

[26] Abrahms, 'Why Terrorism Does Not Work', 56.
[27] Abrahms, 'Why Terrorism Does Not Work', 76–7.

already argued, *Moral Distinction* should also protect civilians against excessive collateral harm.

This is especially relevant to counterinsurgency, since insurgents habitually exploit incumbents' concerns about collateral harm. If they could ignore these concerns, they could often be more effective, at less cost. Counterinsurgencies are fought among civilians; counterinsurgents must trade off risks to their combatants against risks to civilians.[28] Disregarding civilian suffering minimizes friendly casualties. If *Moral Distinction* rested exclusively on the Necessity Argument, then civilians' protection against collateral harm would be considerably weaker than it is now.[29] Indeed, even now the protection of civilians from collateral harm is under serious pressure as belligerents argue that exposing civilians to greater risk is necessary to fight back against an adversary that hides among its civilian population. In Gaza in 2014, for example, Israeli politicians argued that inflicting apparently excessive civilian casualties was an unavoidable element of the only strategy that would prevent Hamas and others from using Israel's moral restraint to their own advantage.[30]

[28] Asa Kasher and Amos Yadlin, 'Military Ethics of Fighting Terror: An Israeli Perspective', *Journal of Military Ethics*, 4 (2005), 3–32; Michael Walzer and Avishai Margalit, 'Israel: Civilians and Combatants', *New York Review of Books* (14 May 2009); Jeff McMahan, 'The Just Distribution of Harm between Combatants and Noncombatants', *Philosophy and Public Affairs*, 38/4 (2010), 342–79; David Luban, 'Risk Taking and Force Protection', in Yitzhak Benbaji and Naomi Sussman (eds), *Reading Walzer* (New York: Routledge, 2014), 230–56.

[29] This is reflected e.g. in soldiers' criticisms of the McChrystal doctrine as applied to ISAF operations in Afghanistan, which placed a greater emphasis on protecting civilians than was typical in the US Army. As one soldier said to the *Rolling Stone* reporter who ended McChrystal's career: 'Bottom line? . . . I would love to kick McChrystal in the nuts. His rules of engagement put soldiers' lives in even greater danger. Every real soldier will tell you the same thing.' Michael Hastings, 'The Runaway General', *Rolling Stone* (8–22 July 2010), 1108–9, <www.rollingstone.com/politics/news/the-runaway-general-20100622>.

[30] Herb Keinon, 'PM: Terrorists Watching Whether World Gives Immunity for Attacks from Schools, Homes', *Jerusalem Post*, 6 Aug. 2014, <www.jpost.com/Operation-Protective-Edge/WATCH-LIVE-Netanyahu-addresses-foreign-press-in-aftermath-of-Gaza-operation-370255>. For my response, see Seth Lazar, 'On Human Shields', *Boston Review* (2014), <http://www.bostonreview.net/world/seth-lazar-human-shields>.

Insurgents too can benefit from inflicting excessive collateral harm on noncombatants, whether directly or by using them as human shields. The Taliban in Afghanistan, for example, achieved significant gains using roadside Improvised Explosive Devices (IEDs).[31] Although IEDs could in theory be used proportionately, in practice they have killed thousands of civilians. A United Nations report notes that 'countrywide, 21 per cent of IED detonations and 46 per cent of suicide attacks resulted in civilian deaths and injuries'.[32] In 2010, IEDs caused 29 per cent of deaths and over 55 per cent of wounds.[33]

As well as ignoring excessive collateral harm, the focus on *indiscriminate* attacks on civilians obscures the potential for selective civilian victimization, especially in terrorism and counterinsurgency. These discriminating anti-civilian attacks can be massive in scale. The Vietcong, for example, selectively assassinated as many as 50,000 people in fifteen years.[34] In the occupation of Ukraine, the Nazis killed as many civilians selectively as they did in massacres.[35] Additionally, detailed research shows that what history calls massacres are often in fact quite selective—as an observer of the 1997 massacres in Algeria noted: 'Massacres are not blind. They are planned and target specific families. They bypass other families.'[36] Terrorists and insurgents also often use selective civilian victimization—witness the rise

---

[31] Does the Taliban have goals that just belligerents could aim at? Their long-term objectives are undoubtedly beyond the pale, but the short-term aim of expelling an occupying military force is the right sort of goal—just think of the anti-colonial wars of the twentieth century.

[32] UNAMA and AIHRC, *Afghanistan: Annual Report on Protection of Civilians in Armed Conflict 2010*, (2011), <http://unama.unmissions.org/Portals/UNAMA/human%20rights/March%20PoC%20Annual%20Report%20Final.pdf>, p. iii. See, further, §2.1 of the report. The report notes that in forty-five incidents where IEDs killed more than five people, less than a third had a discernible military objective as their target.

[33] UNAMA and AIHRC, *Afghanistan*, p. iii.

[34] Kalyvas, 'Paradox of Terrorism', 106.

[35] Kalyvas, 'Paradox of Terrorism', 106. Again, the overarching objectives of the Germans were obviously not those a just belligerent could have aimed at. However, putting a stop to a violent resistance is, I assume, the sort of goal that could be justified.

[36] Quoted in Kalyvas, 'Paradox of Terrorism', 107.

in assassinations of individual noncombatants by the Afghan Taliban in recent years.[37] Research on the effectiveness of selective civilian victimization remains to be done, but it has one obvious advantage over indiscriminate attacks: if your objective is to coerce a target audience into some set of actions, targeting specific civilians who help the adversary gives others clear incentives to defect to your side.[38]

Even if indiscriminate anti-civilian attacks were ineffective in war (and I argue next that they are not), this would not vindicate the Necessity Argument. The same must also be true for excessive collateral harm, and selective civilian victimization. Evidence on the latter remains to be seen, but greater leeway to inflict collateral harm would clearly affect strategic outcomes.[39] Taking precautions to reduce risks to civilians has heavy costs.

Kalyvas, Abrahms, and Pape all define effectiveness by contribution to overall strategic success. They think a tactic is ineffective unless it leads to victory. But this is obviously too restrictive. First, it raises the epistemic burden too high. Wars are confusing. Victory and defeat are overdetermined. It is often hard to tell whether some particular tactic contributed to victory. More importantly, attacks can be effective by achieving an intermediate objective, even if they do not ultimately yield strategic success.[40]

We can see this clearly when those intermediate goals are met, but defeat nonetheless follows. Suppose capturing town X would help us

---

[37] UNAMA and AIHRC, *Afghanistan*.

[38] Downes, 'Draining the Sea', 422. See generally Stathis N. Kalyvas, 'Wanton and Senseless? The Logic of Massacres in Algeria', *Rationality and Society*, 11/3 (1999), 243–85.

[39] See in particular Michael Gross, *Moral Dilemmas of Modern War: Torture, Assassination and Blackmail in an Age of Asymmetric Conflict* (Cambridge: CUP, 2010); Kasher and Yadlin, 'Military Ethics of Fighting Terror'.

[40] Abrahms compounds this error by taking the stated goals of terrorist organizations at face value: seven of the forty-two goals he identifies are 'destroy Israel', alongside hopes to 'sever US–Israel relations', 'sever US–apostate relations', 'spare Muslims from "Crusader Wars"', and 'establish utopian society in Japan', among others. Should we judge terrorist tactics ineffective because they fail to realize a utopia, or should we rather infer that terrorists talk big?

win, and using tactic T_X we do capture it, but because we lose town Y, we lose the war regardless. If this were sufficient to show that T_X was ineffective, then almost all the harms inflicted by the losing side in a war, no matter how justified their goals, would be unnecessary. The same would apply in ordinary life: if I break a murderer's arm in the failed attempt to prevent him from killing me, I harm him unnecessarily and so act impermissibly. These are not acceptable results.

Elsewhere I argue that, for reasons like these, the necessity constraint is best interpreted subjectively rather than objectively, as a function of expected harms and benefits.[41] Indeed, that interpretation is implicit in the working analysis of necessity that I presented earlier. Defending that position in detail here would be a distraction. Instead we need only recognize that military tactics sometimes achieve intermediate goals short of strategic success, which make the tactic count as effective.

Consider asymmetric conflicts in which insurgents or other non-state groups confront a powerful incumbent. Anti-civilian attacks by insurgents can mobilize and galvanize their own community, boosting their side despite the crushing imbalance of power with the adversary.[42] They can attract financial backers, as well as possible fighters.[43] Insurgents might also attack their own community to enforce compliance with their agenda—the Algerian civil war is an example.[44]

Counterintuitively, insurgents can also win international support by victimizing civilians. When small attacks on civilians provoke strong governments to respond disproportionately, insurgents can portray themselves as underdogs, victims of an unfair imbalance

---

[41] Seth Lazar, 'Necessity in Self-Defense and War', *Philosophy and Public Affairs*, 40/1 (2012), 3–44.

[42] Pape, 'Strategic Logic', 345. See also Mia M. Bloom, 'Palestinian Suicide Bombing: Public Support, Market Share, and Outbidding', *Political Science Quarterly*, 119/1 (2004), 61–88.

[43] Bloom, 'Palestinian Suicide Bombing'; Assaf Moghadam, 'Motives for Martyrdom: Al-Qaeda, Salafi Jihad, and the Spread of Suicide Attacks', *International Security*, 33/3 (2008–9), 56–8.

[44] Kalyvas, 'Wanton and Senseless?', 251.

of power.[45] Regardless of whether they achieve overall strategic success—and their battles might be ongoing or might be decided by other factors—provoking the adversary can definitely be effective. The Kosovo Liberation Army, for example, increased solidarity among Kosovar Albanians by attacking Serbian police, provoking vicious crackdowns, which ultimately led to international intervention.[46] Kurdish attacks on Turkish targets prompted government repression, which slowed 'the assimilation of the Kurdish population into Turkish culture', a valuable intermediate goal of Kurdish nationalism.[47] Hindu nationalists have used terrorism to divide Hindus from Muslims in cycles of retaliation.[48] Hamas increased violence before Israel's 1996 and 2001 elections, encouraging support for the right-wing party, Likud, which predictably responded with crackdowns that further galvanized Palestinian resistance.[49]

Anti-civilian tactics by the militant wing of insurgent movements can also enhance their negotiating factions' bargaining power. In this way Irish and Basque nationalists, for example, have forced concessions from their adversaries, including regional autonomy and some degree of political recognition.[50] In Palestine, Hamas activists clearly regarded Israel's withdrawal from the Gaza Strip as a victory achieved by their anti-civilian tactics.[51]

Finally, anti-civilian tactics can contribute to the intermediate goals of insurgency by rendering a territory ungovernable. As the last decade and a half in Iraq and Afghanistan have shown, this is particularly effective against an occupying military force. The incumbent's inability

---

[45] Gray, *Modern Strategy*, 295. This is a prominent theme in US Army, 'Civilian Casualty Mitigation', e.g. 1–17 and 1–21.

[46] Peter Chalk, 'The Evolving Dynamic of Terrorism in the 1990s', *Australian Journal of International Affairs*, 53/2 (1999), 152.

[47] James M. Lutz and Brenda J. Lutz, 'How Successful is Terrorism?', *Forum on Public Policy*, Online (2009), 15.

[48] Sikata Bannerjee, *Warriors in Politics: Hindu Nationalism, Violence, and the Shiv Sena in India* (Boulder, Colo.: Westview Press, 2000), 120.

[49] Andrew H. Kydd and Barbara F. Walter, 'The Strategies of Terrorism', *International Security*, 31/1 (2006), 74.

[50] Gray, *Modern Strategy*, 295–6.

[51] Kydd and Walter, 'Strategies of Terrorism', 63.

to regain control discredits it; it also uses resources on remedial measures, diverting them from prevention.[52]

States too can achieve important intermediate goals through tactics that victimize civilians—strategic success is not the whole story. In counterinsurgency, anti-civilian tactics can reduce friendly casualties—by prioritizing force protection over collateral harms to noncombatants or directly by attacking civilians. Jason Lyall has shown that indiscriminate artillery shelling (at random times, from random locations) by Russian counterinsurgents on Chechen villages reduced rebel attacks between 2000 and 2005.[53] He paired shelled villages with otherwise similar but unshelled villages, to see the difference in insurgent response. One might expect indiscriminate shelling to be counterproductive, leading to more attacks from shelled than from control villages, but Lyall finds the opposite to be true. Shelled villages drop from a mean of 2.11 attacks to 1.5, in the ninety days before and after a Russian strike, while control villages drop from 2.15 to 2.05 during the same period.[54] This means shelling yielded a 24.2 per cent reduction in insurgent attacks.[55] He shows that this translates into eighty-one fewer attacks in the ninety days after shelling than would otherwise have taken place. Since the average insurgent attack killed 0.88 Russian soldiers and wounded another 1.21, the reduction in insurgent attacks attributable to shelling in effect saved seventy-one soldiers' lives, and a further 107 escaped wounding.[56]

---

[52] C. C. Harmon, 'Five Strategies of Terrorism', *Small Wars and Insurgencies*, 12/3 (2001), 57. See also US Army, 'Civilian Casualty Mitigation', 1–17.

[53] Lyall, 'Evidence from Chechnya', 13. Again, as objectionable as the Russian government's treatment of the Chechen people has been, their goal of defeating a violent rebellion is the sort of goal a just belligerent *could* aim at.

[54] Lyall, 'Evidence from Chechnya', 18–19.

[55] Lyall, 'Evidence from Chechnya', 18–19.

[56] Lyall, 'Evidence from Chechnya', 20–1. With a 95% confidence interval, the following ranges apply: 28–136 missing attacks; 25–120 soldiers' lives saved; 34–165 who escaped wounding. NB Lyall found that 'the evidence does not support the claim that violence is redistributed to neighbouring villages' (Lyall, 'Evidence from Chechnya', 24). Jeff McMahan has noted that Lyall's research does not show that it was the anti-civilian component of the Russian shelling that led to the reduction in insurgent attacks—e.g. by deterring the insurgents directly or by leading other civilians to refuse to allow the insurgents to fight from their villages. It is also consistent with the

Civilian victimization can also yield intermediate dividends in interstate conflicts. Although noncombatants do not pose threats, they do contribute to the war effort, as noted in Chapter 1. Killing civilians can diminish the adversary's productive capacity, as well as diverting resources away from offence towards defence.[57] Indeed, these were the goals of the US firebombing of Japan in 1943 and 1944.[58] In short wars the fighting will be over before damage to production capacity can tell. But in wars of attrition, belligerents are more likely to use up their stockpiles of materiel, so civilian productive capacity 'becomes directly relevant to success or failure on the battlefield'.[59]

Finally, civilian victimization can also contribute to overall strategic success, not only to intermediate goals. First, insurgent groups using terrorist methods in asymmetric conflicts can achieve strategic objectives by coercing their more powerful adversaries. These conflicts are often asymmetric with respect to both the belligerents' relative military capacities and their relative commitment to the issue at stake. The weak actor often seeks concessions from the strong that matter profoundly to the weak, but are peripheral to the strong.[60] Although nation-states are resilient when their vital interests are threatened, a disparity of interest makes coercive strategies more

random shelling having killed or injured the insurgents, interdicting future attacks. This is possible, but given that the Russians selected targets at random, without any attempt to identify specific insurgent targets, it is unlikely. The harms done to civilians could be construed as foreseen but unintended, but I think that random firing into civilian areas violates noncombatant immunity, even if it is intended to achieve a military objective.

[57] Benjamin Valentino et al., 'Bear Any Burden? How Democracies Minimize the Costs of War', *Journal of Politics*, 72/2 (2010), 351. See also Barry Watts, 'Ignoring Reality: Problems of Theory and Evidence in Security Studies', *Security Studies*, 7/2 (1997), 154.

[58] Alexander Downes, 'Desperate Times, Desperate Measures: The Causes of Civilian Victimization in War', *International Security*, 30/4 (2006), 152–95.

[59] Valentino et al., 'Bear Any Burden?', 357.

[60] Kenneth F. McKenzie Jr, 'The Revenge of the Melians: Asymmetric Threats and the Next QDR', *Institute for National Strategic Studies, National Defense University*, 62/1 (2000), 4.

effective.[61] Some also argue that democratic states are particularly vulnerable to coercion, since they are more sensitive to casualties.[62]

Pape's research into the effectiveness of suicide bombing between 1980 and 2001 confirms this analysis. In the 1980s, there were thirty-one recorded suicide attacks worldwide; 104 in the 1990s, and fifty-three in 2000–1.[63] Since then this number has rocketed—Afghanistan alone saw 280 suicide attacks between 2009 and 2010.[64] Pape asks what explains this increase, and concludes that suicide terrorism is growing because terrorists justifiably believe that it works.[65] Suicide terrorists fighting the French and US in Lebanon in 1983, Israel in Lebanon in 1985, Israel in the occupied territories in 1994 and 1995, and Sri Lanka since 1990, made more gains after resorting to suicide operations than they did before.[66] Out of eleven campaigns completed in the test period, more than half 'closely correlate with significant policy changes by the target state'.[67] Leaders of terrorist groups, other observers in their community, neutral analysts, and adversary government leaders 'often agreed that suicide operations accelerated or caused the concession[s]'.[68] This is an impressive success rate, considering both the general ineffectiveness of military coercion (effective only 30 per cent of the time, according to Pape)[69] and the paucity of alternative options available to terrorists fighting powerful adversaries. Of course, many of the attacks discussed by Pape were not anti-civilian—the attacks on the US barracks in Lebanon, for example. But some were, and those that were not still reveal the possibility of achieving success through spectacular coercion, which is the basic model for civilian victimization.

---

[61] McKenzie Jr, 'Revenge of the Melians', 3.

[62] Martin Shaw, *The New Western Way of War: Risk-Transfer War and its Crisis in Iraq* (Cambridge: Polity, 2005). See also Paul W. Kahn, 'The Paradox of Riskless Warfare', *Philosophy and Public Policy Quarterly*, 22/3 (2002), 2–8. For the contrary view, see Abrahms, 'Superior Counterterrorists'.

[63] Pape, 'Strategic Logic', 343.

[64] UNAMA and AIHRC, *Afghanistan*, p. iii.

[65] Pape, 'Strategic Logic', 350.   [66] Pape, 'Strategic Logic', 344.

[67] Pape, 'Strategic Logic', 351.   [68] Pape, 'Strategic Logic', 344.

[69] Pape, 'Strategic Logic', 351.

Pape notes that suicide bombing works best when the bomber's objectives are limited and territorial. Ejecting an occupier is easier than overthrowing a government. This applies beyond suicide terrorism. Campaigns of national liberation have often successfully used anti-civilian tactics—witness the anticolonial struggles of the mid-twentieth century, such as the expulsion of (some) colonizers in Cyprus, Palestine, Aden, and Algeria. More recently, many consider Spain's withdrawal from Iraq after the 2004 Madrid bombings a direct success for terrorism.[70] Others counter that Spaniards did not reject the ruling Popular Party because they were cowed by the terrorists, but because of the government's inept handling of the bombings, and its rush to blame them on ETA.[71] But this misses the point: that mishandling would not have occurred without the attack, which aimed not merely to coerce the Spaniards through punishment, but to sow discord and dissent, and invite just such a maladroit response.

Counterinsurgents too can achieve strategic success through civilian victimization in asymmetric conflicts. Insurgents depend on the civilian population for food, shelter, money, and recruits.[72] Sometimes this relationship is even formalized, as insurgents create parallel state structures, including a tax regime.[73] Equally important, noncombatants provide 'human camouflage', enabling rebels to evade detection.[74] Civilians hide weapons and deliver messages for the insurgents. Guerrillas might also rely on civilian institutions, including 'financial, law enforcement, welfare, political, educational, and media institutions'.[75] The media are especially important, as are the

---

[70] Rose et al., 'Does Terrorism Ever Work?', 187.

[71] Rose et al., 'Does Terrorism Ever Work?'.

[72] Hugo Slim, *Killing Civilians: Method, Madness and Morality in War* (London: Hurst, 2007), 190–1.

[73] Downes, 'Draining the Sea', 423.

[74] Benjamin Valentino et al., '"Draining the Sea": Mass Killing and Guerrilla Warfare', *International Organization*, 58/2 (2004), 384. See also Downes, 'Draining the Sea', 423; Wood, 'Rebel Capability', 603; Valentino et al., 'Bear Any Burden?', 355.

[75] Gross, *Moral Dilemmas of Modern War*, 158.

homes and internet cafés from where insurgents' grievances and achievements are broadcast to the world. Blocking this support can critically disrupt insurgent groups, denying them materiel, communication, and safe havens.[76] Civilian support for insurgency can be blocked in three ways: elimination, coercion, and division. Elimination is obvious: you cannot contribute to insurgency if you are dead. Coercion likewise: if civilians fear reprisals, they may learn to dissociate from the rebels. Division arises when civilians come to blame the rebels for inviting government attacks.[77] Underlying each approach is this core metaphor: if Mao was right, and the civilian population is the sea in which insurgent fish swim, then 'the surest way to catch the fish is by draining the sea'.[78]

Alexander Downes offers a compelling analysis of ruthlessly effective civilian victimization in the Second Anglo-Boer War (1899–1902).[79] The Boers were swiftly defeated in conventional combat, and turned to guerrilla warfare. The British responded by burning the Afrikaners' farms, and imprisoning their families. Epidemics in the concentration camps killed over 45,000.[80] The guerrillas were weakened; their leader De Wet admitted that 'had not the English burnt the corn by the thousand sacks, the war could have been continued'.[81] Acting President of Transvaal, Schalk Burger, said that it was 'not the arms of the enemy which directly compelled us to surrender, but…the sword of hunger and nakedness, and…the awful mortality amongst our women and children in the Concentration Camps'.[82]

---

[76] Downes and Cochran, 'Targeting Civilians to Win', 30–1. See also Lyall, 'Evidence from Chechnya', 6.

[77] Wood, 'Rebel Capability', 604; Lyall, 'Evidence from Chechnya', 7.

[78] Valentino et al., 'Draining the Sea', 385. See also Downes, 'Draining the Sea'; e.g. Spain in Cuba, France in Algeria, the Soviets in Afghanistan, and Sudan in Darfur.

[79] Were the British objectives the sort that a just belligerent could aim at? This is a marginal case, but, treated as another instance of an incumbent putting down a rebellion, I think it is close enough.

[80] Downes, 'Draining the Sea', 422.

[81] Quoted in Downes, 'Draining the Sea', 434.

[82] Downes, 'Draining the Sea', 437.

The Italians used similar tactics when suppressing the 1923–32 Sanusi uprising in Cyrenaica (now Libya).[83] After seven years of 'fruitless pursuit', they interned the entire population. The rebels had been well-supported, and the civilians' imprisonment both removed this support and offered brutal leverage: between 85,000 and 100,000 entered the camps, but only 35,000 survived. These concentration camps were 'probably the key to [Italian] victory in Cyrenaica'.[84] Similar tactics paid dividends for the US in the Philippines at the turn of the twentieth century.[85]

Anti-civilian tactics were clearly effective in South Africa and Cyrenaica. Perhaps the British and Italians had aims that just warriors could not aim at—if it is necessary to lock up so much of the population to subdue them, then the counterinsurgent project may be illegitimate. But just counterinsurgencies sometimes face a robust insurgent movement, and if these tactics have worked in the past, they may well work again.[86]

Civilian victimization can also yield strategic results in interstate conflicts. Sieges, for example, have a long history of success. Consider the sieges of Paris in the Franco-Prussian War, Plevna in the Russo-Turkish War, Adrianople in the First Balkan War, and Beirut in the Lebanon War.[87] The most significant success is probably the Allied blockade of Germany and Austria-Hungary in the First World War, which may have caused 400,000 civilian deaths, but surely hastened the German surrender.[88] As with sieges, so with nuclear bombardment: even Pape concedes that the threat of nuclear attack is a decisive coercive tool.[89]

---

[83] Downes, 'Draining the Sea', 427.

[84] E. E. Evans-Pritchard, quoted in Downes, 'Draining the Sea', 427.

[85] Downes, 'Draining the Sea', 422. For more examples see Lyall, 'Evidence from Chechnya', 6.

[86] Thanks to Jeff McMahan for pressing me on this point.

[87] Downes and Cochran, 'Targeting Civilians to Win', 54.

[88] Downes and Cochran, 'Targeting Civilians to Win', 54. For the number see Valentino et al., 'Bear Any Burden?', 352.

[89] Robert Pape, *Dying to Win: The Strategic Logic of Suicide Terrorism* (New York: Random House, 2005), 75.

Additionally, the forced removal of a civilian population can itself be a military objective when territorial control is at stake.[90] When two states contest a territory in which part of the population shares characteristics with the dominant groups in each state, eliminating or evacuating the civilians affiliated with the opponent can contribute directly to securing territorial control.[91] It reduces potential threats from those civilians, removing a seat of resistance, as well as a potential trigger for a future rescue by the adversary.[92] And it facilitates forming a cohesive nation-state with a stronger claim to the territory, based on facts of occupation.[93] The Arab/Israeli conflict is a particularly salient example. Downes cites a Zionist leader saying in 1938 'we cannot start the Jewish state with...half the population being Arab...Such a state cannot survive even half an hour.'[94] Expelling the Arab population from their villages was almost certainly wrong, but it clearly helped to establish a Jewish state.[95] Perhaps a just belligerent could not aim at this sort of objective, but I doubt it: there can surely be just colonization, whether or not this is an example.[96]

Lastly, large-scale quantitative research into the strategic effectiveness of civilian victimization over the last two centuries suggests that it is at least as effective as exclusively counterforce tactics in wars of attrition.[97] Working from their dataset of around 200 conflicts over

[90] Downes, 'Draining the Sea', 420.

[91] Alexander Downes and Kathryn McNabb Cochran, 'It's a Crime, But is it a Blunder? The Efficacy of Targeting Civilians in War', unpublished MS, 10.

[92] Downes, 'Desperate Times', 154.

[93] Downes, 'Desperate Times', 167; Downes and Cochran, 'Targeting Civilians to Win', 47–8.

[94] Downes, 'Desperate Times', 167.

[95] Downes, 'Desperate Times', 167. One might also think of the Balkan states' expansion into areas controlled by the Ottoman Empire in 1912–13, the Israeli war of independence, and Turkey's intervention in Cyprus in 1974: Downes and Cochran, 'Targeting Civilians to Win', 31–2.

[96] For one argument that colonization can be justified in very limited historical circumstances, see Chaim Gans, *A Just Zionism* (Oxford: OUP, 2008).

[97] Obviously a dataset such as this does not allow for differentiating between belligerents according to their objectives. Nonetheless these are interesting and relevant results.

200 years, Downes and Cochran find that 'civilian victimisation was probably an important component of victory in 30 per cent of the wars of attrition (29 per cent of states) and at least partially contributed to victory in 45 per cent of such wars (50 per cent of states)'.[98] They then observe that 'relative to the rates of victory for states or sides that did not target noncombatants in wars of attrition—40 per cent—civilian targeting is not radically less (or more) effective than fighting more conventionally'.[99] As I argue in the next section, states victimize civilians when they are already on the ropes and have few other alternatives. We should therefore expect anti-civilian tactics to correlate (much) more often with defeat than with victory.[100] Valentino et al. agree: belligerents 'are most likely to resort to killing civilians in the most difficult and desperate conflicts—when conventional military means are ineffective or too costly', so we can predict that 'victory in these circumstances will be relatively unlikely no matter what tactics a combatant employs'.[101] If states that victimize civilians in interstate wars achieve the same rate of success as those that do not, that itself strongly implies that attacking civilians is militarily effective.

5. But Can it Be Necessary?

The preceding sections have shown that civilian victimization can be effective in insurgencies and terrorist campaigns, counterinsurgency, and interstate armed conflict. It follows that if belligerents have no other effective options besides anti-civilian tactics, then those tactics satisfy necessity, and the Necessity Argument cannot explain why killing civilians is worse than killing soldiers. In this section, I show that such situations can arise in terrorist campaigns and insurgencies, counterinsurgency, and interstate conflicts.

---

[98] Downes and Cochran, 'Targeting Civilians to Win', 55.
[99] Downes and Cochran, 'Targeting Civilians to Win', 55.
[100] Downes and Cochran, 'It's a Crime, But is it a Blunder?', 21.
[101] Valentino et al., 'Bear Any Burden?', 375–6.

Insurgents usually have other options besides civilian victimization to counter occupying forces. The stronger actor generally has a significant military presence in the disputed territory, so the insurgents have many targets besides civilians. In Iraq and Afghanistan, for example, insurgents' counterforce tactics were very effective—partly owing to the occupying powers' discomfort with military casualties.[102] Moreover, sometimes in asymmetric conflicts nonviolent resistance is more likely to succeed than either form of military response.[103] The question is not, however, whether anti-civilian tactics are generally the only means to prosecute insurgencies, but whether sometimes nonviolent and counterforce alternatives are not available or, if available, are not effective. Nonviolent measures are, of course, always available. But it would surely take an idealist to think that they are always likely to succeed. Nonviolent resistance relies on one's adversaries being susceptible to moral pressure. Often they are not. Sometimes force must be used. Why might anti-civilian tactics be available when counterforce ones are not?

Simply put, because it is much easier to launch a terrorist campaign than a guerrilla war.[104] Confronting an adversary's armed forces requires resources, personnel, and training that an insurgent group may lack. Direct confrontation would end the insurgency swiftly. Attacking targets that cannot fight back is much easier to do.[105] And it is very hard to defend a whole population against a few determined individuals (particularly when they are prepared to lose their lives).[106] Fewer than twenty primary operatives carried out the 9/11 attacks; the ten Mumbai attackers held India's economic capital

[102] Scott Sigmund Gartner and Gary M. Segura, 'War, Casualties, and Public Opinion', *Journal of Conflict Resolution*, 42/3 (1998), 278–300; Shaw, *Western Way of War*.

[103] Erica Chenowith, *Why Civil Resistance Works: The Strategic Logic of Nonviolent Conflict* (New York: Columbia University Press, 2011).

[104] Herfried Münkler, *The New Wars* (Cambridge: Polity, 2002), 109.

[105] McKenzie Jr, 'Revenge of the Melians', 6; Pape, 'Strategic Logic', 346. See also Slim, *Killing Civilians*, 158; Münkler, *The New Wars*, 111.

[106] Pape, *Dying to Win*, 75–6.

to ransom for a day, killing 164 people; the Oklahoma bomber, Timothy McVeigh, acting with one accomplice, killed 168 and injured 450 others. We have already seen that civilian victimization in insurgencies can be effective; now we see that it is easier and less costly than are counterforce measures. Sometimes the resources, personnel, and training required for an effective guerrilla campaign are lacking, but anti-civilian tactics are still possible. In these cases, civilian victimization becomes necessary.

In general, counterinsurgents need not use anti-civilian tactics. Contemporary counterinsurgency doctrine favours winning hearts and minds, gathering intelligence, and focusing on targeted (and high-tech) counterforce measures.[107] Again, however, we want to know not whether civilian victimization is *always* necessary, but whether it is sometimes the only option left.

Fighting cleanly means taking on additional costs. Winning hearts and minds requires enormous financial resources, personal risks, and a diplomatic skill-set that soldiers predictably lack.[108] Confining attacks to adversary combatants is especially difficult when they hide among a civilian population from which they are indistinguishable.[109] Sometimes there are no military targets to hit; for example, Michael Gross observes that in the 2006 Hezbollah/Israel war, Hezbollah had only eighty-three command posts, which were destroyed within five days. Hezbollah continued to strike, but there was no way to strike back, he argues, apart from aiming at the civilian institutions on which Hezbollah relied.[110] When civilian support for insurgents is high enough that hearts-and-minds tactics are doomed to fail, and when the insurgents hide among civilians and civilian objects, counterforce tactics can prove very costly, in both lives and resources.[111] If anti-civilian tactics are less costly than counterforce measures, then sometimes civilian victimization will be the only option.

---

[107] This is particularly clear in US Army, 'Civilian Casualty Mitigation'.
[108] Valentino et al., 'Draining the Sea', 384, 403.
[109] Valentino et al., 'Draining the Sea', 384.
[110] Gross, *Moral Dilemmas of Modern War*, 158.
[111] Valentino et al., 'Draining the Sea', 384, 403.

Well-supported insurgencies are difficult to defeat; all options are poor—even for strong states. Civilian victimization can be effective, it risks little harm to the ruling side (civilians cannot fight back), and civilians are an easy target—'essentially immobile, almost impossible to conceal, and difficult for the guerrillas to defend'.[112] If counterforce measures fail, or become too costly, anti-civilian tactics might be the only options left. In the Boer War and the Sanusi uprisings, for example, the British and Italians turned to anti-civilian tactics only after their counterforce measures had failed.

Research by Valentino et al. shows that this trend applies generally. Using a dataset of 147 wars between 1945 and 2000, they ask why some states killed civilians *en masse* (defined as intentionally killing more than 50,000 over five years or less).[113] Mass killing is most likely, they show, when states face grave threats from an adversary that depends on the civilian population and has successfully repelled conventional attacks.[114] Conflicts against guerrilla opponents who posed a major threat saw a six-fold increase in the likelihood of mass killing; where guerrillas were strongly supported by civilians, mass killings were eight times more likely.[115] When guerrillas both posed a major threat and were well supported, mass killings were eighteen times more likely.[116] Although they note that mass killings rarely seem to work,[117] Valentino et al. conclude that, when states attack civilians:

less violent strategies for counterinsurgency have proven at least equally costly and prone to failure...For leaders determined to stave off defeat and unwilling to make major political concessions to the opposition, therefore, mass killing simply may appear as the most attractive choice among a set of highly unattractive options.[118]

[112] Valentino et al., 'Bear Any Burden?', 355.
[113] NB this is a narrower variable than 'civilian victimization'—not only intentional attacks, but on a massive scale. Also note that with such a large dataset we cannot differentiate among belligerents according to their objectives.
[114] For their research design, see Valentino et al., 'Draining the Sea', 387ff.
[115] Valentino et al., 'Draining the Sea', 394.
[116] Valentino et al., 'Draining the Sea', 397–8.
[117] Valentino et al., 'Draining the Sea', 401.
[118] Valentino et al., 'Draining the Sea', 402–3.

In other words, states kill civilians *en masse* because their leaders believe it necessary. This should be a chilling conclusion for those who think necessity grounds the protection of civilians in war. They may respond that, given the historical record, these beliefs were unreasonable. However, the paucity of viable alternatives and examples such as Chechnya, the Anglo-Boer War, the Sanusi uprising, and the Philippines all tell against this argument.

In interstate conflict, the same general reasons apply. Civilian victimization is easy, because the target cannot defend itself or hide. Counterforce measures are hard. When counterforce measures fail, as they often do, anti-civilian tactics may be the only option left. Even in Pape's analysis of British bombing of German cities in the Second World War, he notes that the British started bombing civilians only after attempts to target military objectives (for example, by flying during the day) had failed or proved too costly.[119] Even if the new strategy was ultimately unsuccessful, the lack of viable alternatives might have allowed it to meet necessity, ex ante.[120]

Valentino et al. back up this general observation with specific data, showing that states attack civilians when they face great threats and think they have no other options. Looking at all interstate wars between 1900 and 2003, they conclude that the decision to target civilians is based on 'incentives…created by the risks, threats, and opportunities associated with the particular conflict'.[121] Killing noncombatants 'is often a calculated military strategy'.[122] Even in war 'few states actively desire to kill enemy civilians in large numbers. But in certain circumstances combatants may come to believe that doing so is the best way to achieve victory at an acceptable cost.'[123]

---

[119]   Pape, *Bombing to Win*, 269.

[120]   See Downes, 'Desperate Times', 164. See also Valentino et al., 'Bear Any Burden?', 537.

[121]   Benjamin Valentino et al., 'Covenants without the Sword: International Law and the Protection of Civilians in Times of War', *World Politics*, 58 (2006), 340.

[122]   Valentino et al., 'Covenants without the Sword', 340.

[123]   Valentino et al., 'Covenants without the Sword', 350.

According to their analysis, states fighting wars of attrition or counterinsurgency 'killed nearly six times more civilians than did states utilising other strategies'.[124] When attrition and counterinsurgency combine, the predicted number of civilian casualties jumps exponentially; when these combine with a long war and maximalist war aims, the numbers increase still more.[125] The inference is clear: when states fight longer, more arduous wars, where the threats they face are grave, and where counterforce measures prove ineffective, they are more likely to attack civilians, as a desperate measure that might be intrinsically unattractive, but is preferable to accepting defeat.[126]

As with the same arguments in counterinsurgency, this should worry advocates of the Necessity Argument. Clearly, states target civilians in war because they believe that doing so is effective, and that they have no other option—in other words, because they believe that killing civilians is necessary. If necessity grounds the protection of noncombatants in war, then it denies them protection when they need it most.

One might respond that the leaders' *beliefs* about necessity are irrelevant—what matters is whether anti-civilian tactics were *in fact* necessary.[127] This raises some interesting and complex questions that I cannot do justice to here.[128] However, two brief responses are possible.

First, regardless of how we should best interpret the necessity constraint, we should be troubled that it provides so weak a bulwark against political and military leaders who believe attacking civilians to be necessary. If this were the best argument for *Moral Distinction*, we would have to keep it secret, because it is so vulnerable to abuse by political leaders who believe attacking civilians will be effective when their other options fail.[129]

---

[124] Valentino et al., 'Covenants without the Sword', 371.
[125] Valentino et al., 'Covenants without the Sword', 371.
[126] Valentino et al., 'Covenants without the Sword', 371.
[127] Thanks to Jeff McMahan and a reviewer for pressing me on this.
[128] I consider them in depth in Lazar, 'Necessity in Self-defense and War'.
[129] I owe this objection to a reviewer for *Review of International Studies*.

Second, if the necessity constraint is applied ex post, assuming all the facts are known, then it would have radical implications for the permissibility of killing combatants in war.[130] Objectively, many combatants killed in war die pointlessly—killing them neither averts a specific threat, nor helps avert the overall threat posed by their state. Even for those whose deaths have some use, there was almost certainly some available alternative action that would have had the same result, but done less harm. And if your side loses the war, then all of the deaths it caused were unnecessary, and hence impermissible. We face a dilemma. On an objective, ex post standard, most of the killing done by both just and unjust combatants in war is unnecessary, so impermissible. But on a subjective, ex ante standard, killing civilians clearly can be necessary, and the Necessity Argument protects civilians least when they need it most.

6. Conclusion

Killing civilians is often utterly wanton, and this helps explain why it is so seriously wrongful. Firebombing Dresden probably contributed little, if anything, to strategic success in the Second World War. The same is true for the nuclear devastation of Hiroshima and Nagasaki. By contrast, killing soldiers is usually instrumental to achieving your operational goals. At least, killing enough of them is usually sufficient for military victory. These are important points, and they do help buttress *Moral Distinction*.

But the Necessity Argument has clear limits. It does not explain why killing civilians is worse than killing soldiers in the pursuit of an unjustified aim. It cannot explain why collaterally killing civilians is worse than killing soldiers. And killing civilians is often effective in war, when no other options are available.

What's more, even when the Necessity Argument does get the right deontic verdicts, we must surely wonder if it does so for the right

---

[130] For a similar observation, see Daniel Statman, 'Can Wars Be Fought Justly? The Necessity Condition Put to the Test', *Journal of Moral Philosophy*, 8/3 (2011), 435–51.

reasons.[131] The visceral opposition that we feel in response to attacks on civilians is not adequately captured by the complaint that they were ineffective—as though our reactions would switch if only they had been strategically successful. When we confront anti-civilian violence, we do not ask, 'but did it _work_?' Indeed, I have argued that the very reason these attacks tend to be ineffective stems from the moral condemnation that they invariably inspire. To be true to these judgements, we need to explain the intrinsic wrongfulness of anti-civilian attacks. The Necessity Argument cannot help with this.

Ultimately, I think we should not lean too heavily on the Necessity Argument. It has the air of wishful thinking—like the belief that cheats never prosper, or that the best way to help others is to help yourself. On this view, the protections that civilians enjoy in war are scarcely even constraints, since they never remove options that belligerents really had to take. The moral reality of war is not so accommodating: hard choices are the rule, not the exception. And we need arguments for *Moral Distinction* that will protect civilians even when killing them is expedient.

---

[131] Thanks to Lachlan Umbers and Adil Haque for pressing me to emphasise this point.

3

Opportunistic and Eliminative Killing

1. Introduction

In a market in Rawalpindi, in the summer of 2006, I was drinking tea with a silk trader when a man sat down next to me and pulled out his cellphone. He gestured for me to look. From his smile, I thought he wanted to show me something funny. But when I looked down, I saw a pixelated, 1.5 by 1.5 inch video of the beheading of Daniel Pearl. Pearl's murderers—Ahmed Omar Saeed Sheikh and three accomplices—killed him in 2002, ostensibly to coerce the American government into releasing prisoners from Guantanamo Bay. But they were really courting notoriety, sowing discord and terror, and issuing a rallying cry. Pearl's body was the medium into which they carved their defiance at the world. My neighbour on the bench was just another messenger.

It is one thing to kill an innocent person. It is another to treat him as a prop in your horror show, a resource that you can use to advance your own ends. When the Allies firebombed Dresden, they aimed to break the will of the German people, so that they would rise up against the Nazis and end the war. The people who burned to death were treated as opportunities, clay to be moulded to Arthur Harris's design. When the British imprisoned the Boers in the first concentration camps, they used the Afrikaners' families to bring the commandos to heel. Each death was a message: your revolt is costing your wives and children their lives.

These tactics have been used throughout history, though they reached their twin apotheoses in the aerial bombings of the mid-twentieth century and the instantly global beheadings of the twenty-first. Mankind has plumbed new depths in its capacity for mass slaughter, and for sensationalizing innocent deaths. Most often, these measures are used against civilians. They are treated as a resource, an opportunity to advance their killers' ends. The killer gains a benefit from their deaths that he would not otherwise have enjoyed. This is *opportunistic* killing.[1]

Killing soldiers is often quite different from this. They are not tools to be used; they are obstacles, threats. Their killers only achieve goals by killing them that they could have secured just as easily in their victims' absence. This is *eliminative* killing.

If opportunistic killing is worse than eliminative killing, and if civilians but not soldiers are killed opportunistically in war, then that would help explain why killing civilians is worse than killing soldiers.[2]

2. Opportunistic and Eliminative Killing

Each individual is an end in herself; she is not just a site for the realization of value.[3] The fact that we could realize more value overall by harming someone, or depriving her of a benefit, does not entail

---

[1] Others use different labels for opportunistic killing, and subdivide the general category into different subcategories. I stick with Quinn's labels because these are terms of art, and I would gain little by rebadging them. See Victor Tadros, *The Ends of Harm: The Moral Foundations of Criminal Law* (Oxford: OUP, 2011); Helen Frowe, *Defensive Killing* (Oxford: OUP, 2014).

[2] Arguments like this have been hinted at before, but never developed in detail. See Jeff McMahan, *Killing in War* (Oxford: OUP, 2009): 226; Jeff McMahan, 'Who is Morally Liable to Be Killed in War?', *Analysis*, 71/3 (2011), 553; Tadros, *Ends of Harm*, 244.

[3] This idea has always been at the heart of deontological ethics, but my adaptation of it is most proximately informed by the work of Warren S. Quinn, esp. 'Actions, Intentions, and Consequences: The Doctrine of Double Effect', *Philosophy and Public Affairs*, 18/4 (1989b), 334–51; 'Actions, Intentions, and Consequences: The Doctrine of Doing and Allowing', *Philosophical Review*, 89 (1989a), 287–312.

that doing so is permissible. Respecting someone's moral status means acknowledging that sometimes we may not maximize value at her expense.

For some this is normative bedrock. For others, we can dig deeper: individuals are ends in themselves because we are autonomous, rational agents, with our own plans for life and a capacity for acting morally.[4] We are not mere sites for the realization of value, because we each have our own lives to lead.[5] Our autonomy and our capacity for acting morally make us the kinds of beings whose interests are worth protecting, over and above their impartially considered worth.

However we understand the foundations of this principle, its implications for ethics are clear. When distributing benefits and burdens, we are prohibited from making marginal interpersonal trade-offs.[6] For example, I cannot justify imposing a cost of degree x on you simply by the fact that it realizes a benefit y (where $y \geq x$) for me, or for some other person. As Rawls puts it, this approach ignores the 'separateness of persons'.[7] Costs that I incur myself can be fully offset by benefits to me of the same size, but costs imposed on one person cannot be fully counterbalanced by same-sized benefits received by another.

This simple idea is at the heart of deontological moral and political philosophy. It underpins our right to sometimes forgo maximizing the good, as well as principles of distributive justice, and those governing permissible harm. In particular, it is the foundation of the non-comparative theory of liability to defensive harm introduced in Chapter 1. On that view, it is not enough that the outcome in which Victim kills Threat is *very slightly better* than the outcome in which Victim lets herself die. There must be a relevantly substantial

---

[4] Rawls's discussion of Kantian and political conceptions of the person is relevant here: John Rawls, *Political Liberalism* (Chichester: Columbia University Press, 1996).

[5] The connection between moral status and autonomy, which of course has deep Kantian roots, has recently been nicely drawn out in Tadros, *Ends of Harm*, 122.

[6] I'm not suggesting that this is an absolute or unconditional prohibition—there may be exceptions.

[7] John Rawls, *A Theory of Justice* (Oxford: OUP, 1999).

difference between these outcomes, for Threat to lose her right not to be killed.

We always have reason to treat innocent people as ends in themselves. Sometimes we needlessly fall short of this standard; sometimes exigent circumstances mean that we have to. We can do this in different ways; all involve treating the victim as a means, by imposing costs on her to the advantage of others. Treating innocent victims as a means like this is always *pro tanto* wrongful. But there are degrees of moral seriousness. How you instrumentalize your victim and your reasons for doing so determine the severity of that wrong.

In this chapter, I focus on the distinctive moral seriousness of *opportunistic* killing.[8] When you kill a victim opportunistically, you derive a benefit from harming her that you would not have enjoyed in her absence. That is, you fail to treat her as an end in herself, *not only* in the sense that you see her as, at most, a site for the realization of value, but you also *actually use her*. Her presence affords you an opportunity to advance your goals. When Ahmed Omar Saeed Sheikh beheaded Daniel Pearl, he not only treated Pearl as though his interests and standing were morally irrelevant, but also used his death to cow enemies and inspire allies. Sheikh could not have achieved those goals without using Pearl (or someone like him) like that.

This basic idea—or something close to it—can explain common opposition to the various kinds of harm that deontologists typically think particularly hard to justify.[9] Consider the man who is pushed in front of the trolley to bring it to a halt, the innocent person used as a human shield, or the healthy victim of the utilitarian surgeon who

---

[8] Although I disagree with them (and they disagree with each other) on many details, my understanding of opportunistic and non-opportunistic agency is informed by my reading of Quinn, 'The Doctrine of Double Effect'; Jonathan Quong, 'Killing in Self-Defense', *Ethics*, 119/2 (2009), 507–37; Tadros, *Ends of Harm*. It also owes much to Gerhard Øverland's work, esp. 'Moral Obstacles: An Alternative to the Doctrine of Double Effect', *Ethics*, 124/3 (2014), 481–506.

[9] These cases are now so familiar to those working on the ethics of harm as to be clichéd, and I will not reproduce them in detail. If anyone reading this book is encountering them for the first time here, I would love to hear from you! Tweet me @sethlazar.

harvests his organs to save five lives. Each is harmed in a way that draws a benefit from the harming, which the beneficiary could not have enjoyed in the absence of the victim. This helps explain why these acts are so seriously objectionable.

Conversely, if we hold the goals sought constant, then killing someone non-opportunistically is less seriously wrongful (as long as the target is innocent, it is always wrongful to some degree). Suppose I kill an enemy soldier, who is rushing at me with a bayonet. I am no better off by killing him than I would have been had he not been there. The same is true if I shoot an innocent person who is blocking my escape from a bloodthirsty enemy.

Non-opportunistic killing is really defined by what it isn't, so it is hard to settle on a less unwieldy name. But the familiar term is *eliminative*, and it just about fits the bill. When I kill you eliminatively, I am aiming only at ends that I could just as easily have realized had you been absent. Rather than treating you as a resource that I can use, you are instead a problem that killing you solves, or eliminates. The word sounds rather chilling, but then, there is something positive about opportunity, so these implications should not mislead us!

My understanding of eliminative killing is somewhat unusual. Other philosophers think that eliminative and opportunistic agency are subsets of intentional agency.[10] But I think that eliminative killing can be unintended (perhaps opportunistic killing can as well, though it seems less likely). If we bomb a military target to advance our just cause and foreseeably kill some nearby civilians as a result, then we derive no benefit from killing them that we would not have had in their absence. If I save the five by diverting the trolley down the side track, where it kills one, then I (and the five) have gained nothing from killing the one that I would not have had if the track had been empty. These are species of eliminative harm, which helps explain why they are easier to justify than opportunistic harms.

[10]   McMahan, *Killing in War*, 170; Tadros, *Ends of Harm*: 14; Quinn, 'The Doctrine of Double Effect'; Quong, 'Killing in Self-Defense'.

Indeed, the eliminative/opportunistic agency distinction might even supplant that between intention and foresight. It certainly deals better with some cases than does the more familiar distinction. Consider this sequence, for example:[11]

Bunker 1: Ten Islamic State militants are taking cover in a bunker. An innocent civilian is trapped nearby.
Bunker 2: The militants have grabbed the civilian and hauled him into their bunker; you're able to tell them apart.
Bunker 3: The militants have disguised the civilian so there is no way to tell the difference between them and him.
Bunker 4: The militants are attempting to flee the bunker. They have disguised the civilian and he is running with them. You cannot tell which is which.

Suppose you're a Peshmerga fighter, and the militants pose an imminent, serious threat. In *Bunker 1–3*, your only means of killing the militants is by firing a missile that will surely kill the civilian too. In *Bunker 4*, you have a rifle, and are able to kill the eleven people one by one. Three observations seem immediately plausible. First, if it is permissible to fire in *Bunker 1*, it should be permissible in *2* and *3* as well. Second, if it is permissible to kill all eleven in *3*, then it should be permissible to kill all eleven in *4* too.[12] Third, as we progress through the cases, it becomes harder and harder to say that you do not intentionally kill the civilian. In *Bunker 1*, you aim at the militants in the bunker, and the civilian's death is a clear side-effect of your action. In *Bunker 4*, you aim at the civilian, trying to lethally wound him with your rifle. You do not intentionally [kill an innocent civilian]. But you do intentionally kill this person, and this person is a civilian. It stretches credulity to assert that your intentions are no different here from what they are in *1*.

Examples like these cause (perhaps surmountable) trouble for the intention/foresight distinction. But the lens of eliminative agency

[11] Adapted from McMahan, 'Morally Liable'.
[12] For more on this conundrum, see Seth Lazar, 'In Dubious Battle: Uncertainty and the Ethics of Killing', unpublished MS (2014).

makes perfect sense of them. The civilian is harmed eliminatively each time. You derive no benefit from his presence that you would not have had in his absence. So you wrong him less seriously than you would have if you had harmed him opportunistically. Suppose, for example, that you sight the militants by targeting the civilian (perhaps they are all camouflaged, but he is wearing a bright tracksuit). *Then* you would be killing him opportunistically, which would stand out as worse than killing the civilian in *Bunker 1–4*.

However, I do not want to press the point. Intentions may be independently relevant to permissibility, and indeed to how we should understand opportunistic agency. I mean simply to point out one salient kind of eliminative killing that will be important later.

Opportunistic killing is worse than eliminative killing when your aims are good ones—winning a just war, averting a threat to innocents. But it is also worse when your aims are either trivial or nefarious. Contrast the beheading of Daniel Pearl with the combat killing of a Peshmerga guerrilla by IS militants, in the battle for Erbil, 2014. Pearl's murderers' goals were as bad as those of the Islamic State. And yet it seems clear that the murder of Pearl is worse than that of the hypothetical guerrilla, in part because Sheikh and his group made such egregious use of their victim, whereas the militants derive no benefit by killing the guerrilla that they would not have enjoyed in his absence. They are not using him in the same way.

Similarly, contrast two murders by a serial killer. The first slakes his bloodlust, the second silences a potential witness. Killing someone to gratify oneself is even worse than killing him to eliminate a justified threat. Though the second is still seriously bad—after all, it amounts to treating the victim as though neither his standing nor his interests matter at all—it is not as objectionable as using another human being for one's own gratification. Of course, what the serial killer does is *so* seriously wrongful that these differences are perhaps swamped. But still, he wrongs the victim that he uses more gravely than the one he does not.

Holding the aims constant, opportunistic killing is worse than eliminative killing. This has implications for both liability and lesser evil justifications for harm.

The central idea of the non-comparative account of liability is that, since we are not mere sites for the realization of value, there must be some substantial asymmetry between the potential bearers of a harm for it to be permissible to kill another person to save oneself. The magnitude of this asymmetry may vary depending on how one is going to harm the target. The grounds for liability to being oppor- tunistically killed might be more exacting than those for liability to being eliminatively killed.

Even for eliminative killing, the asymmetry must still be substan- tial. The target is not merely a site for the realization of value, so it is not acceptable to kill her just because doing so yields a marginally better state of affairs, impersonally construed, than letting yourself die. But the outcome in which you kill her opportunistically is worse than the one in which you kill her eliminatively. So for it to be permissible to bring this outcome about, rather than let yourself be killed, the asymmetry between yourself and the target might have to be greater. In other words, someone could be sufficiently responsible for an unjustified threat to be liable to be killed elim- inatively, though not responsible enough to be liable to be killed opportunistically.[13]

I want this book to be ecumenical between different theories of liability, and to stay relatively clear of the arcana of different theories of self-defence. So, beyond the general observation that the threshold for liability to be killed must be high, I do not want to endorse too precise an account of what makes one liable. Nonetheless here is a possibility, which I shall merely float, and defend elsewhere: for a person to be liable to eliminative killing, she needs to at least have acted subjectively impermissibly in a way that is substantially causally connected to an unjustified threat that another person now faces, which can be averted by killing her. For her to be liable to opportun- istic killing, she must be *culpable* for a substantial causal contribution.

---

[13] This kind of possibility is discussed in: Frowe, *Defensive Killing*; McMahan, *Killing in War*; Tadros, *Ends of Harm*.

This reflects how opportunistic killing increases the burden of justification.

Less controversially, opportunistic agency is relevant to lesser evil justification in a similar way. To justify killing an innocent person opportunistically, you need to achieve more good than if killing him is eliminative. This is one reason why it's harder to justify pushing the man into the path of the trolley than it is to justify flipping the switch and sending the trolley down the side track, where it kills one person. You're using the one, but not the other, so you must achieve more for it to be permissible.

Philosophers typically invoke the contrast between opportunistic and eliminative agency to explain the permissibility of killing non-responsible threats. Suppose an innocent man has been thrown down a well towards you; if you do not vaporize him with your ray gun, he will crush you to death.[14] Most philosophers think that killing the falling man is permissible; one can explain this by arguing that you kill him eliminatively: you would be just as well off if he were to simply disappear.

But this approach to the falling man case invites objections, which might cast doubt on the moral significance of the eliminative/opportunistic agency contrast. Critics invoke another hypothetical scenario that seems also to involve eliminative killing, but in which they think killing is impermissible. Suppose you can save yourself from an onrushing train only by hiding in an alcove, but the alcove is presently occupied, and can fit only one person. Luckily you still have your ray gun from that unfortunate time in the well.[15] Most philosophers think that vaporizing the man in the alcove is wrong. But you would clearly be no better off for killing him than you would be if he were absent from the alcove. So it looks like eliminative killing.

[14] Robert Nozick, *Anarchy, State and Utopia* (Oxford: Basil Blackwell, 1974).

[15] Judith Jarvis Thomson, 'Self-Defense', *Philosophy and Public Affairs*, 20/4 (1991), 291.

Some respond by trying to show that killing the falling man really is materially different from killing the man in the alcove.[16] For my part, I think the two cases are indeed morally identical, and that killing is impermissible in both of them, even though it is not the worst kind of killing that you can do. I acknowledge that most people think killing the falling man is permissible, but none of the justifications for that conclusion resolve this basic problem: the outcome in which you survive and he dies is no better than one in which he survives and you die. You cannot treat him as a mere site of value, and kill him just to save yourself, unless there is a relevantly substantial asymmetry between you. There is no such asymmetry. Though it is better to kill the falling man than to use someone as a human shield or kill her for her organs, it is still impermissible.

I do think, however, that your killing eliminatively is relevant to justifying your actions as a lesser evil. It might be permissible to kill the falling man, and the person in the alcove, if you were saving, say, four lives besides your own. Whereas if you were killing opportunistically, you would need to save (many) more lives to have a lesser-evil justification.

Two further clarifications are in order. First, the idea of opportunistic agency uses a counterfactual: you derive a benefit from harming the person that you would not have enjoyed in her absence. But what does this mean? It does not mean 'had she never existed', since perhaps something she did in the past might be crucial to your surviving now, and anyway working out how the world would be had she never existed is impossible to do. Instead, I invite you to imagine this scenario: as you are deciding what to do, your potential victim disappears. Vanishes. If you could not achieve your goal in her absence, then harming her is harder to justify, because it is opportunistic.

This is not the only possibility. Jonathan Quong argues that we should imagine that the victim, *and her property*, were spirited away.[17] Since he thinks that we own the space that we occupy, this

---

[16] Quong, 'Killing in Self-Defense'.   [17] Quong, 'Killing in Self-Defense'.

means killing the person in the alcove is opportunistic, since if she and her property were absent, the alcove would be inaccessible. I reject this view for two reasons: I am sceptical that we have property rights over the space that we occupy; and I am even more sceptical that property rights are relevant to the ethics of killing. When life and death are at stake, property rights pale into insignificance. But I will hold back from this particular rabbit hole. The arguments offered in this chapter would work equally well on Quong's account of opportunistic agency.

Second clarification: suppose that if a serial killer had not murdered Andrew, he would have satisfied his bloodlust by killing Bill. Does this mean he has not killed Andrew opportunistically, because had Andrew not been there he would have killed Bill?[18] It does not. The reference made to Andrew when describing the wrongfulness of the serial killer's opportunistic agency is not strictly *personalized*. What matters is that he derived a benefit that he could not have had in the absence of some person playing the Andrew role, who happens in this case to be Andrew.

3. War

Opportunistic killing is worse than eliminative killing. If killing civilians in war is more often opportunistic than killing soldiers, then that affords *Moral Distinction* real support. Of course, this argument would not cover all cases. It could not explain why collaterally killing civilians is worse than collaterally killing soldiers, for example, since neither kind of killing is typically opportunistic. But it could help justify *Moral Distinction* for intentional killing. And it could do so neutrally, for both just and unjust combatants. Or at least, it could do so if its minor premise were true. Although the waters are certainly muddy and it is hard to generalize, I think that it is.

---

[18] For discussion of a similar example, see Øverland, 'Moral Obstacles'.

In Chapter 2, I noted that strategic theorists draw a distinction between 'denial' and 'punishment' strategies.[19] Denial strategies deny the adversary victory on the battlefield. Punishment strategies coerce the adversary into surrender by inflicting heavy losses off the battlefield. Punishment strategies are primarily opportunistic; denial strategies primarily eliminative.

Punishment strategies reached their peak with the advent of aerial bombing. In *Command of the Air*, Douhet argued that subjecting an adversary to 'merciless pounding from the air' with conventional explosives, incendiaries, and poison gas would lead to 'a complete breakdown of the social structure', so that 'to put an end to horror and suffering, the people themselves, driven by the instinct of self-preservation, would rise up and demand an end to the war'.[20] Aerial bombing of civilian population centres during the Second World War (by both sides), and in the conflicts in Korea and Vietnam, was conceived on this model.[21]

Punishing civilians to coerce their leaders has also been key for both sides of insurgencies and other asymmetric conflicts. The British imprisonment of Afrikaner civilians in the Second Anglo-Boer War is a particularly chilling example, as was the Italian treatment of the Sanusi in Cyrenaica.

Unfortunately, civilians in insurgencies tend to take fire from both sides. The insurgents often punish noncombatants to enforce compliance with their cause and deter collaboration with the incumbent. Witness, for example, the assassinations of individual civilians by the Afghan Taliban in recent years, or the attacks on police recruits there and in Iraq, or indeed the 50,000 Vietnamese executed by the North Vietnamese Army during the Vietnam War.[22] Insurgents also

[19]   Robert Pape, *Bombing to Win: Air Power and Coercion in War* (London: Cornell University Press, 1996).
[20]   Quoted in Alexander Downes and Kathryn McNabb Cochran, 'Targeting Civilians to Win? Assessing the Military Effectiveness of Civilian Victimization in Interstate War', in Erica Chenowith and Adria Lawrence (eds), *Rethinking Violence: States and Non-State Actors in Conflict* (Cambridge, Mass.: MIT Press, 2010), 27.
[21]   Pape, *Bombing to Win*.
[22]   UNAMA and AIHRC, *Afghanistan: Annual Report on Protection of Civilians in Armed Conflict 2010* (2011), <http://unama.unmissions.org/Portals/UNAMA/human

use attacks on civilians affiliated with the incumbent population to coerce their leaders into concessions. These were particularly familiar during the anticolonial wars of the mid-twentieth century; their contemporary descendants are terrorist attacks such as 9/11 and the Bali, London, and Madrid bombings.[23] And of course the recent spate of beheadings by Islamic State constitute opportunistic killing in its purest, most malevolent form.

Many of the anti-civilian measures employed to achieve intermediate strategic objectives are also relevant here. Consider, for example, attacking civilians to provoke their government into a disproportionate response, thus garnering for the attacker international and domestic support as the underdog. Or consider attacks aimed at rendering an occupied territory ungovernable. Each death is just another way to show that the occupier cannot guarantee the most fundamental prerequisites of political life.[24]

Killing civilians is often opportunistic. When it is, this helps explain why it is so seriously wrong. But we are trying to defend a comparative thesis. If killing soldiers is just as opportunistic as killing civilians, then this argument fails to support *Moral Distinction*.

Killing soldiers in war is almost always in part eliminative. In general, when soldiers kill enemy combatants in war, they achieve goals that they could have realized in their enemies' absence. Enemy combatants always constitute a problem, which is solved by killing them. This is for two reasons. First, many enemy combatants are threats. Even those who are not dangerous now may be so in the future. Even when this does not ground liability to be killed, it does mean that, if we kill them, that killing is at least somewhat eliminative.

Obviously not all enemy combatants are threats. As noted in Chapter 1, many contribute little if anything either to threats to

%20rights/March%20PoC%20Annual%20Report%20Final.pdf>; Stathis N. Kalyvas, 'The Paradox of Terrorism in Civil War', *Journal of Ethics*, 8/1 (2004), 106.

[23] e.g. Hugo Slim, *Killing Civilians: Method, Madness and Morality in War* (London: Hurst, 2007), 148–9.

[24] C. C. Harmon, 'Five Strategies of Terrorism', *Small Wars and Insurgencies*, 12/3 (2001), 57. See also US Army, 'Civilian Casualty Mitigation', *Army Tactics, Techniques and Procedures*, 3–37.31 (2012), 1–17.

individuals or to overall threats to states. And yet, killing them is also to some extent eliminative. Recall *Bunker 3* and *4*: when an innocent person is intermingled with liable targets, you derive no benefit from killing the innocent person that you would not have had in his absence. It's just that you cannot kill the liable ones unless you kill the innocent one as well. The same is true for soldiers: we cannot tell which of the enemy combatants are dangerous and which are not, and we cannot kill the dangerous ones unless we kill the non-threatening ones.[25] But in killing the non-threatening ones, we are no better off than we would have been had they simply been absent— we would then have been able to target the dangerous ones exclusively.

Killing soldiers is almost always in part eliminative, while killing civilians is often in part opportunistic. Obviously, however, that is not the whole story. In interstate conflicts, although noncombatants do not pose threats, they do contribute in many ways to the war effort. Killing civilians can diminish the adversary's productive capacity, so one is not profiting from their presence, but eliminating their contribution to the enemy threat.[26] According to internal military documents from 1943 and 1944, for example, the American firebombing of Japan was not a punishment strategy.[27] Rather, the objective was to destroy Japan's dispersed system of industrial production and to generate a labour shortage by killing workers.[28] Of course, in short wars the fighting is over before damage to production capacity can

[25] Seth Lazar, 'The Responsibility Dilemma for *Killing in War*: A Review Essay', *Philosophy and Public Affairs*, 38/2 (2010), 180–213.

[26] Benjamin Valention, Paul Huth, and Sarah Croco, 'Covenants without the Sword: International Law and the Protection of Civilians in Times of War', *World Politics*, 58 (2006), 351; Barry Watts, 'Ignoring Reality: Problems of Theory and Evidence in Security Studies', *Security Studies*, 7/2 (1997), 115–71.

[27] Alexander Downes, 'Desperate Times, Desperate Measures: The Causes of Civilian Victimization in War', *International Security*, 30/4 (2006), 152–95.

[28] Similarly, in response to Chinese intervention in the Korean War in early Nov. 1950, US bombers targeted civilian populations to create a *cordon sanitaire* between the Chinese border and UN lines.

start to tell. But in drawn-out wars of attrition, belligerents are more likely to use up their stockpiles of materiel, so, as I argued in Chapter 2, civilian productive capacity 'becomes directly relevant to success or failure on the battlefield'.[29]

Anticolonial insurgencies and movements for national liberation have often used anti-civilian violence to remove enemy civilians from an occupied territory. The settlers' presence is the problem that violence is aimed to redress.[30] The same applies when two states contest a territory inhabited by a mixture of sympathizers of each state. Removing the civilian population affiliated with the opponent can contribute directly to securing territorial control, reducing potential threats from those civilians, and removing a trigger for future rescue missions.[31]

Finally, in counterinsurgency, the incumbent often attacks noncombatants to deprive the insurgent of popular support. In Chapter 2 I discussed how insurgents depend on the civilian population for food, shelter, money, recruits, and 'human camouflage'.[32] Although counterinsurgents undoubtedly often rely on opportunistic tactics—seeking to coerce the civilian population by making an example of some—there is scope here for harming noncombatants eliminatively as well.[33]

As for killing combatants: we can plausibly argue that, in war, *all* killing of combatants is at least also opportunistic. Victory is achieved not by killing every individual who contributes to a threat against us, but by communicating to the enemy armed forces and their

[29] Valentino et al., "Covenants without the Sword', 357.

[30] Alexander Downes, 'Draining the Sea by Filling the Graves: Investigating the Effectiveness of Indiscriminate Violence as a Counterinsurgency Strategy', *Civil Wars*, 9/4 (2007), 420.

[31] Alexander Downes and Kathryn McNabb Cochran, 'It's a Crime, But is it a Blunder? The Efficacy of Targeting Civilians in War', unpublished MS (2011), 10.

[32] Slim, *Killing Civilians*, 190–1 Benjamin Valentino et al., '"Draining the Sea": Mass Killing and Guerrilla Warfare', *International Organization*, 58/2 (2004), 384. See also Downes, 'Draining the Sea', 423; Reed M. Wood, 'Rebel Capability and Strategic Violence against Civilians', *Journal of Peace Research*, 47/5 (2010), 603; Valentino et al., 'Covenants without the Sword', 355.

[33] Kalyvas, 'Paradox of Terrorism'.

leadership, through the losses we inflict, that the costs of continuing to fight outweigh the expected advantages of doing so. When we kill an enemy combatant we derive a benefit from him that we could not have had in his absence (except by harming someone else in the same way): we send a message to our enemies. Killing in war is always *pour encourager les autres.*

We might miss this opportunistic dimension to killing in war if we consider this argument at the collective level. When one state attacks another, which then defends itself, in a sense the latter gains nothing through that defence that it would not have had in the absence of the aggressor state. The harm done appears eliminative. But even at the collective level violence in war is always also opportunistic: it is justified in part by the importance of deterring future aggression. If the defender does not respond robustly to this attack, then it is left more vulnerable in the future. Again, this means using the enemy combatants as a means to convey a message to other potential aggressors that their actions will not be tolerated.

All the harms that we inflict in war convey a message to current and future aggressors: that the costs of attacking us outweigh the benefits. This strategic opportunism is matched at the tactical level. By killing enemy combatants, we can make the survivors fear for their lives, leaving them preoccupied with protecting themselves rather than advancing their attack. We can draw resources away from the defence of our other objectives by imposing heavy losses here. And we can sow confusion among the enemy, breaking up their chain of command. Each of these seems to be basic to the art of warfare; each involves using the victims of lethal force as a resource to avert threats posed by others.

This is especially clear in asymmetric conflicts, in which weaker belligerents use opportunistic tactics as a force-multiplier. In situations where they cannot repel the adversary by mere force of arms, they seek to force concessions by raising the costs of fighting.[34]

---

[34] What Robert Pape says of suicide terrorism is true of asymmetric tactics more generally: 'The common feature of all suicide terrorist campaigns is that they inflict

Consider the attacks on the American barracks in Lebanon in 1984, the Mogadishu killing of fourteen Delta Force operatives in 1994, or indeed the improvised explosive devices that were so effective against coalition forces in Iraq and Afghanistan.[35] These examples lay bare how counterforce attacks can be used as a means to exert political pressure.

So, all killing in war involves an opportunistic dimension. But the very generality of this thesis weakens its claim to undermine this argument for *Moral Distinction*. True, all killing in war is also opportunistic. That is one reason why wars are so hard to justify. But still, intentionally killing civilians is *more* opportunistic than intentionally killing soldiers; and killing soldiers almost always involves an eliminative dimension. Each kind of killing involves mixed kinds of agency. But the mixture in anti-civilian violence is more opportunistic than it is for counterforce attacks. So the generalization that killing civilians is worse than killing soldiers is borne out.

I noted in Chapter 1 that, because I endorse a high threshold of responsibility for liability, my argument for *Moral Distinction* would be essentially disjunctive. Killing civilians is worse than killing soldiers, either because the civilians are innocent and the soldiers are not or because killing innocent civilians is worse than killing innocent soldiers. I think the argument from opportunistic agency better supports this defence of *Moral Distinction* than the alternative, grounded in a low threshold of responsibility for liability. Suppose you think that a low degree of responsibility is sufficient to render one liable to be opportunistically killed. And suppose that, as a result, many civilians are liable to be opportunistically killed in war. Then the argument from opportunistic agency would not help explain why

punishment on the opposing society, either directly by killing civilians or indirectly by killing military personnel in circumstances that cannot lead to meaningful battlefield victory.' Robert Pape, 'The Strategic Logic of Suicide Terrorism', *American Political Science Review*, 97/3 (2003), 346.

[35]   Kenneth F. McKenzie Jr, 'The Revenge of the Melians: Asymmetric Threats and the Next QDR', *Institute for National Strategic Studies, National Defense University*, 62/1 (2000).

killing civilians is worse than killing soldiers, because if the members of two groups are all liable to be opportunistically killed, then killing them in this way does not wrong them, so killing them in any less objectionable way does not wrong them either. There is no morally relevant difference between eliminatively killing a liable soldier and opportunistically killing a civilian who is liable to that fate.

4. Conclusion

Everyone with moral status deserves to be treated as an end in herself, not just as a site for the realization of value. When we do make trade-offs, we can carry them out in more and less objectionable ways. The worst way is to use a person to achieve some end, deriving a benefit from her presence that you could not have had in her absence. This kind of opportunistic harming is distinctly objectionable. It contrasts with eliminative harming, which leaves the agent no better off than he would have been had his victim not been present. The collateral killing of noncombatants in war is primarily eliminative. So opportunistic agency can underpin only a version of *Moral Distinction* that is confined to intentional killing. And it does provide *Moral Distinction* with real support, especially for the subordinate thesis that intentionally killing innocent civilians is worse than intentionally killing innocent soldiers. All killing in war is somewhat opportunistic. That is one reason why wars are such moral tragedies. But there are degrees of opportunism within this, and some of the goals achieved by killing combatants could have been realized had they simply been absent. Killing combatants almost always has an eliminative dimension. Killing civilians, by contrast, only sometimes counts as eliminative. Instead, the norm is for civilians' deaths to be used, as Daniel Pearl's was, to sow panic among the adversary population, and to send a bloody message to their leaders.

4

Risky Killing

1. Introduction

On 22 July 2005, police officers from Specialist Firearms Command, a branch of the London Metropolitan Police, followed Jean Charles de Menezes onto an underground train at Stockwell Tube Station. Subsequent inquiries have not yielded a settled account of what followed, but all agree that de Menezes was shot seven times in the head and once in the shoulder, at close range, having done nothing more to raise the officers' suspicions than to stand up. The officers trailing de Menezes believed him to be Osman Hussein, involved in a failed bombing attempt the day before. They also subsequently claimed to have believed him to be a proximate threat. As the truth has emerged, however, we have seen that the grounds for thinking de Menezes either to be Hussein or to be an imminent threat were flimsy at best. The officers who killed him took an extraordinary risk in discharging their weapons. Many factors contributed to making this such an execrably unjust killing, but their readiness to risk violating an innocent man's right to life is one of the most important.

No single property matters more to the ethics of killing than the target's degree of responsibility for contributing to an unjustified threat. This alone can remove all taint involved in killing, by justifying a limited prescription of his right to life. On some theories of liability, there are other necessary conditions that must also be satisfied, but even for them, responsibility is what justifies liability. But this poses a problem, because it is so difficult to know, in war, who is responsible for unjustified threats and who is not. We are almost always unsure whether the threats we would avert are unjustified, whether and to what extent our prospective targets contributed to those threats, and whether they were culpable for those contributions. Each of these facts helps determine if and how far one's target is liable. Given this pervasive uncertainty, whether you kill the innocent in war is often a matter of luck. All killing in war involves taking very serious risks with your victims' rights.

On a high-threshold account of liability to be killed in war, civilians are only very rarely liable, while many soldiers who contribute to unjustified aims in war will be liable. Killing innocent civilians there-fore involves taking a greater risk with their rights to life than does killing innocent soldiers. Had the officers who killed de Menezes had better grounds to believe him a lethal threat, then they would still have violated his rights by killing him, but they would have wronged him less severely in doing so. Their violation of his right to life would have been objectively less morally grave. Killing civilians is objectively worse than killing soldiers, because it involves taking a greater risk of killing an innocent person.

2. Risky Killing

Objective probabilities—chances—are mind- and perspective-independent features of the world, like the 50:50 chance that a radium atom will decay within 1600 years.[1] Evidential probability is the probability justified by a body of evidence. On the best accounts, evidence gives an intuitive, though imprecise, degree of support to the hypothesis in question.[2] Subjective probability is the probability assigned by a subject.[3] Evidential and subjective probabilities are

---

[1] Rachael Briggs, 'The Metaphysics of Chance', *Philosophy Compass*, 5/11 (2010), 938–52.

[2] Timothy Williamson, *Knowledge and its Limits* (Oxford: OUP, 2000), 223; Roger White, 'Evidential Symmetry and Mushy Credence', *Oxford Studies in Epistemology* (Oxford: OUP, 2009), 173.

[3] e.g. F. P. Ramsey, 'Truth and Probability', in Antony Eagle (ed.), *Philosophy of Prob-ability: Contemporary Readings* (London: Routledge, 2010), 52–94; Bruno De Finetti, *Theory of Probability: A Critical Introductory Treatment* (Chichester: Wiley, 1990).

both species of epistemic probability, indexed to a particular epistemic position.

In this section, I defend the following thesis:

Risky Killing: when A kills B, and B is not liable to be killed, other things equal A's act is *pro tanto* more seriously fact-relative wrongful the higher the epistemic probability,[4] when she acted, that B was not liable to be killed.

In other words, riskier killings are worse than less risky killings.

To build a case for *Risky Killing*, it will help to have some examples in mind. Consider:

Sniper-Low: Aggie is a sniper, hunting Charlie, a terrorist whose death will save lives. She has a man in her sights. Her evidential and subjective probability that this is *not* Charlie are both 0.1. She fires. She kills Bruce, who was in fact innocent.
Sniper-High: The same as *Sniper-Low*, except that Aggie's evidential and subjective probability that this is *not* Charlie are high—say 0.9.[5]

Aggie's act is worse in *Sniper-High* than in *Sniper-Low*, because it was so much likelier that her target was innocent.[6] Many will share this intuition. Aggie took a bigger risk with Bruce's life in *Sniper-High* than in *Sniper-Low*, so of course she wronged him more seriously if she kills him! Indeed, some will find *Risky Killing* more convincing than any argument in its favour. However, in this section I offer three arguments to persuade those who are not already on board. I then address what follows when Aggie's evidence and her beliefs diverge, before stating *Risky Killing* in its canonical form.

An agent's mental states when violating a right can affect the seriousness of that right-violation.[7] Intended rights-violations are

---

[4] This is intentionally ambiguous between the two kinds of epistemic probability—more on this later.

[5] These cases raise some interesting issues that I lack space to address here. In particular, I focus on fact- rather than evidence-relative wrongfulness, and discuss only the probability of innocence, rather than also considering the probability that killing her target is unnecessary or disproportionate.

[6] For simplicity, assume that Aggie is justifiably certain that if this is not Charlie, then it is an innocent person.

[7] This claim is rejected by, among others, Judith Jarvis Thomson, 'Self-Defense', *Philosophy and Public Affairs*, 20/4 (1991), 283–310; Frances M. Kamm, 'Failures of

worse than unintended ones; killing an innocent person for one's gratification is worse than killing him to save others' lives; killing him opportunistically is worse than killing him to eliminate a threat that he himself poses.[8] In the same spirit, I think violating someone's right to life when one believes one's act will probably violate that right is worse than doing so when that outcome is less likely.

To see why, consider a paradigm wrongful killing: Aggie is certain that Bruce is innocent, but intentionally cuts his throat, to satisfy a whim. By killing Bruce like this, she shows herself ready to violate his most fundamental right for a trivial end. This shows total disregard for his standing as her moral equal, someone with moral status whom she cannot use to fulfil her whims. Now vary the likelihood that Bruce is innocent—suppose there is some probability that killing him will avert a lethal threat to an innocent victim. The less likely this possibility, the more likely it is that Bruce is innocent. If Aggie nonetheless proceeds, then she proves herself proportionately readier to sacrifice him for her own trivial goals, and she more gravely insults his moral standing.

One might object that Aggie does not disrespect Bruce in the *Sniper* cases since, unlike in the paradigm case, her aim is noble: to save Charlie's victims.[9] Suppose we stipulate that Charlie's potential victims are numerous enough that proceeding, at least in SNIPER-HIGH, is subjectively permissible. How can Aggie disrespect Bruce if she does what she subjectively ought to do?

Even if the stakes are high, Aggie disrespects her victim more gravely in *Sniper-High* than in *Sniper-Low*, by proving herself readier to sacrifice an innocent person for the greater good. Even if one's act

Just War Theory: Terror, Harm, and Justice', *Ethics*, 114/4 (2004), 650–92. For excellent defences, see Russell Christopher, 'Self-Defense and Defense of Others', *Philosophy and Public Affairs*, 27/2 (1998), 123–41; Victor Tadros, *The Ends of Harm: The Moral Foundations of Criminal Law* (Oxford: OUP, 2011), ch. 7.

[8] Warren S. Quinn, 'Actions, Intentions, and Consequences: The Doctrine of Double Effect', *Philosophy and Public Affairs*, 18/4 (1989), 334–51; Tadros, *Ends of Harm*.

[9] I owe this objection to a reviewer for *Ethics*.

is all things considered permissible, if it imposes on someone else a cost that she is not required to bear, one disrespects her by treating her as a resource to use or sacrifice for others' sakes.[10] This explains why justifying such impositions is hard, and why marginal interpersonal trade-offs are wrong. The higher the probability that her target is innocent, the more seriously Aggie instrumentalizes him, showing disregard for his moral status as an end in himself. This basic principle applies whether her ends are noble, trivial, or pernicious.

In this chapter I focus on probability of innocence, but we could run the same argument for probability of necessity (see Chapter 2). When you kill an innocent person, the less likely it was that killing this individual would be necessary to achieve some suitably worthwhile goal, the more serious your violation of her right to life, since the higher the risk you have chosen to run of killing this person pointlessly.

The second argument for *Risky Killing* focuses on the choice between harming those who are more and less likely to be innocent. Consider:

Sniper-Choice: The same as *Sniper-Low*, except that Aggie can choose between two targets, each of whom she believes could be Charlie. The probability that the first (call him Bruce-Low) is not Charlie is 0.1; the probability that the second (Bruce-High) is not Charlie is 0.9. Both Bruce-Low and Bruce-High are in fact innocent.

The necessity constraint on defensive force prohibits inflicting unnecessary harm, even on someone who might otherwise be liable.[11] It depends on the truism that all harm is bad (except perhaps when deserved) and so should be minimized. This reasoning extends

---

[10] Victor Tadros argues that it is permissible to sacrifice an innocent person's life for the greater good, when that person would be required to sacrifice his own life for that end (Tadros, *Ends of Harm*, 129). I favour a different view: we have an agent-centred prerogative not to sacrifice our own lives for others' sakes. It can therefore be permissible to kill someone to achieve an objective that she would not, because of her agent-centred prerogative, be required to sacrifice her own life to realize.

[11] See e.g. Seth Lazar, 'Necessity in Self-Defense and War', *Philosophy and Public Affairs*, 40/1, 3–44.

beyond actual harms to risks of harm: if a defensive act involves an unnecessary risk of harm, then that too counts against it, however the risk turns out. Moreover, this extends even more forcefully to risks of *wrongful* harm, since wrongful harms are worse than otherwise similar non-wrongful harms. In other words: if we should minimize harm, then we should minimize risks of harm; and if we should minimize risks of harm, we should minimize risks of wrongful harm.

Whether Aggie shoots Bruce-High or Bruce-Low, she inflicts the same risk of harm (she is a crack shot, certain to hit her target). But if she shoots Bruce-High, then the probability that he is innocent is higher, so she inflicts a higher risk of wrongful harm than if she shoots Bruce-Low. Killing Bruce-High therefore inflicts an unnecessary risk of wrongful harm on him. Aggie could have had the same opportunity to kill Charlie, at a lower risk, by killing Bruce-Low. Killing Bruce-High is worse than killing Bruce-Low, because it breaches the necessity constraint on defensive force.

Riskier wrongful killings are worse violations of the right to life than are less risky killings. I also think they breach a further right, not to be exposed to unchosen risks of wrongful harm; for short, the right not to be endangered. The argument has four stages.

Stage 1: Endangerment is wrongful even if the risks imposed do not lead to harm.[12] Speeding through a residential neighbourhood or conducting brain surgery while drunk are wrong, even if one avoids a collision or removes the tumour. And riskier behaviour is, other things equal, worse than less risky behaviour. If driving through a suburb at 60mph is wrong, doing so at 150mph is still worse; if operating while tipsy is wrong, doing so while smashed is still more so. A few sceptics aside, most philosophers—and most legal jurisdictions—concur that we have a right not to be exposed to unchosen risks of wrongful harm.[13]

---

[12] See Madeleine Hayenhjelm and Jonathan Wolff, 'The Moral Problem of Risk Impositions: A Survey', *European Journal of Philosophy*, 20/S1 (2012), 26–51.

[13] Sceptics: Judith Jarvis Thomson, *Rights, Restitution, and Risk: Essays in Moral Theory* (Cambridge, Mass.: Harvard University Press, 1986); Kenneth Simons, 'When is Negligent Inadvertence Culpable?', *Criminal Law and Philosophy*, 5/2 (2011),

Stage 2: Divide an instance of endangerment into time stages. At T_1, Driver recklessly enters a neighbourhood at 100mph, knowing there are people around, including two pedestrians, Lucky and Unlucky; at T_2, Driver's car hits Unlucky, killing her. Lucky escapes unharmed. Lucky's right against endangerment was violated at T_1. Lucky and Unlucky were in the same position at T_1. So if Driver violated Lucky's right not to be endangered, then he also violated Unlucky's. At T_2 Unlucky suffers a second right-violation, this time of her right to life.

In general, if one person violates another's right then, whatever happens afterwards, *she has still violated that right*. Later events might justify that violation, or restore the status quo ante through compensation. But nothing after a right-violation can make it as though it never happened. Of course, violating someone's right to life is worse than violating his right not to be endangered. When the two occur together, we naturally focus on the more serious right-violation. This is especially clear, for example, with murder. In no case, however, does a second right-violation vitiate an earlier one.

One might worry about how to individuate wrongful impositions of risk. Suppose Driver is doing laps around a block. Does he violate the pedestrians' rights against endangerment each time he passes them?[14] I think their rights protect the pedestrians against the Driver acting in a certain way. Whether he violates their right each lap depends on how we individuate the relevant acts. I cannot properly address such a big topic here. I simply claim that, however we individuate his acts, Driver *does the same thing* to Lucky and Unlucky at T_1. That he then *does something else*, violating another of Unlucky's rights, does not remove a complaint that she would have had, had he not violated that second right.

97–114. Supporters: Michael J. Zimmerman, 'Risk, Rights, and Restitution', *Philosophical Studies*, 128/2 (2006), 285–311; John Oberdiek, 'The Moral Significance of Risking', *Legal Theory*, 18/3 (2012), 339–56; Stephen Perry, 'Risk, Harm, Interests, and Rights', in Tim Lewens (ed.), *Risk: Philosophical Perspectives* (New York: Routledge, 2007), 190–210.

[14] I owe this objection to a reviewer for *Ethics*.

Stage 3: In Stages 1 and 2 the agent imposes a risk of harm on someone who we know is not liable. My primary interest, however, is in risks of suffering *wrongful* harm, when the harm is certain, but liability is in doubt. I must show that intuitions about one carry over to the other.

They do. What matters for this argument, and indeed those already presented, is that the agent has imposed a *risk of wrongful harm*. By showing herself readier to impose that risk in *Sniper-High* than in *Sniper-Low*, Aggie shows greater disrespect for Bruce. By choosing to fire at Bruce-High rather than Bruce-Low in *Sniper-Choice*, she runs an unnecessary risk of inflicting wrongful harm on her victim. And for endangerment, the same principles apply.

Consider again Jean Charles de Menezes. Killing this man was egregiously wrongful, in part because it was so likely, when the officers acted, that he was innocent. They took a terrible risk with an innocent man's rights. But they shot him point-blank in the head: their act was sure to be lethal. They wrongfully endangered de Menezes because they lacked adequate grounds to believe him liable.[15]

Stage 4: The first three stages should persuade anyone who already thinks we have a right against endangerment that it is relevant to Aggie's wrongdoing in *Sniper-High*. For any remaining sceptics, sketching a theory of that right may help.[16]

The right against endangerment has roots in our interest in security, which is both instrumentally and non-instrumentally valuable. Security is the avoidance of unchosen risks of wrongful harm. Enjoying security is instrumental to enjoying other goods.[17] If I am secure, then I escape harms that might otherwise have befallen me. Being

---

[15] There were also many prior instances of gross negligence in this case: see 'Seven Mistakes that Cost De Menezes his Life', *Independent*, 13 Dec. 2008, <www.independent.co.uk/news/uk/crime/seven-mistakes-that-cost-de-menezes-his-life-1064466.html>.

[16] These are attractive alternatives: Perry, 'Risk, Harm, Interests, and Rights'; Oberdiek, 'The Moral Significance of Risking'. For a view with some parallels to my own, see Jonathan Wolff and Avner De-Shalit, *Disadvantage* (Oxford: OUP, 2007), ch. 3.

[17] See, e.g., Hayenhjelm and Wolff, 'The Moral Problem of Risk Impositions'.

insecure also generates anxiety and distress. Besides upsetting us in the present, insecurity makes it more difficult to plan, by closing off options because of the risks involved.[18] For hedonistic and preference-satisfaction theories of well-being, these instrumental goods exhaust security's value. For objectivist theories, there is more to say.

First, I am better off if my freedom from wrongful harm does not avoidably depend on luck. Luck is antithetical to control: if my avoiding some outcome depends on luck, then I cannot control whether that outcome will come about. Control, in turn, is one constituent of autonomy—being autonomous implies having some control over how one's life goes.[19] Being autonomous is non-instrumentally valuable; most of us aspire to this ideal for its own sake, not because of other goods it brings us. Since having control is a way of being autonomous, having control should be non-instrumentally valuable too. Moreover, control over whether one suffers wrongful harm is especially important, given how central our interest in not being wrongfully harmed is. Suppose two people never suffer wrongful harm, one through good choices, the other through sheer luck. The one who had control was better off than the lucky one, just in virtue of having that control.

Obviously though, we cannot avoid luck in all aspects of our lives. But being secure reduces exposure only to one kind of luck: *unchosen risks of wrongful harm*. Even though luck is inescapable, if others avoidably make us dependent on it for our avoidance of wrongful harm, they harm us. Suppose a friend tells you how to walk home at night, in a city that you don't know. He could send you through a safe neighbourhood or through one where late-night muggings are

---

[18] Oberdiek, 'The Moral Significance of Risking'; Stephen John, 'Security, Knowledge and Well-Being', *Journal of Moral Philosophy*, 8/1 (2011), 68–91.

[19] This is especially clear on Pettit's theory of freedom as non-domination, but is also a plausible development of Raz's account of autonomy. See Philip Pettit, 'Freedom and Probability: A Comment on Goodin and Jackson', *Philosophy and Public Affairs*, 36/2 (2008), 206–20; Joseph Raz, *The Morality of Freedom* (Oxford: Clarendon Press, 1986).

common. He chooses to send you through the dangerous neighbourhood. Even if you get home unharmed, you've still been made worse off by having been avoidably placed at risk of wrongful harm. When you find out what he did, you should definitely have words. Life is fragile enough without people adding to the risks we face. Of course, sometimes we enjoy exposing ourselves to risk, like when we skydive, or catch a minibus in Angola. This does not undermine our security, because these risks are *chosen*.

Second, when I am secure, others are robustly disposed not to wrongfully harm me, across a range of possible scenarios. Being the object of their concern is non-instrumentally valuable even if those scenarios never arise. For example, in a just society others protect me against destitution and crime. That my fellow citizens care enough about my well-being to provide such protections is good for me, even if I never call on them. Similarly, a loving family still further protects me, so that through life's vicissitudes I can rely on their support—I enjoy this good even if my life never turns south.[20] When a person is secure, she enjoys a similar status. If others who could harm her if they chose to are robustly disposed not to inflict risks of such harm on her, they protect her, which is valuable even if situations where she might suffer such harm never arise.

To summarize: being secure is instrumental to realizing important benefits, like freedom from anxiety and the ability to plan; it gives us more control over an important part of our lives, so is a non-instrumentally valuable constituent of autonomy; and it means that we have a non-instrumentally valuable status among those who preserve our security. These are weighty interests; but they ground rights only if they impose reasonable costs on the duty-bearers. If we had to avoid imposing *any* risks on others, then we could not live a

---

[20] I draw here on arguments made in Seth Lazar, 'A Liberal Defence of (Some) Duties to Compatriots', *Journal of Applied Philosophy*, 27/3 (2010), 246–57. My current inflection on them is much informed by conversations with Philip Pettit and Nic Southwood, as well as: Philip Pettit, *The Robust Demands of the Good* (Oxford: OUP, 2015); Nicholas Southwood, 'Democracy as a Modally Demanding Value', *Nous*, Online first (2013).

recognizable modern life—we could not drive or fly; we would have to quarantine ourselves when sick, and so on.[21] Our interest in security does not provide a blanket right against all risks, and sometimes it can be outweighed. However, permissible risks are typically slight, in terms of either the degree or the likelihood of threatened harm. Beyond that fair distribution of risks within a society, the right against endangerment is stringent.

Thus far, I have assumed that Aggie's beliefs and her evidence align. However, sometimes her evidence will warrant one view about whether her victim is liable, her beliefs another. Which determines the seriousness of her wrongdoing?

This question raises some interesting and complex problems. To keep things simple, I will focus only on what I need to defend *Moral Distinction*.[22] This means showing that each of my arguments works with Aggie's (sincere, sane) subjective probabilities, but that if she believes Bruce less likely to be liable than her evidence warrants, that gives further grounds for complaint against her when she kills him.

The argument from disrespect works only with subjective probabilities: we cannot infer Aggie's readiness to instrumentalize her victim from facts of which she was unaware or connections that she did not draw, but only from her (sincere, sane) beliefs. The other two arguments work either with subjective or with evidential probabilities. Insofar as Aggie disrespects Bruce-High by inflicting on him an unnecessary risk of wrongful harm, her subjective probabilities are salient. But even if her beliefs and evidence diverge, she still subjects

---

[21] See e.g. James Lenman, 'Contractualism and Risk Imposition', *Politics, Philosophy and Economics*, 7/1 (2008), 99–122; Sven Ove Hansson, 'Ethical Criteria of Risk Acceptance', *Erkenntnis*, 59/3 (2003), 291–309.

[22] There are also interesting overlaps between these questions and those to do with the relationship between belief-relative, evidence-relative, and fact-relative permissibility (on which see Derek Parfit, *On What Matters* (Oxford: OUP, 2011), ch. 7; Tadros, *Ends of Harm*, ch. 11). However, my probabilistic arguments are merely one constituent in a theory of permissibility; the implications of different theories of probability for normative ethics are independent of the implications of the different senses of permissibility.

him to an unnecessary risk of wrongful harm since, relative to Aggie's evidence, she could have taken a lesser risk by killing Bruce-Low, without reducing her probability of achieving her goal. As for endangerment: only when others believe they are imposing risks of wrongful harm do they impugn one's status as the object of others' concern. But it is also bad for others to subject me to risks of wrongful harm on their evidence, even if they do not believe they are imposing such risks.[23]

Each argument works with the agent's subjective probabilities. But what if she believes Bruce less likely to be liable than her evidence warrants? To answer this, we must first know what counts as her evidence. I think evidence is available to an agent when she would have it if she did the morally required research. The evidential probability is the probability that the agent *ought to assign* to an outcome coming about.[24] If the stakes are high—for example, if she is trying to find out if a building is empty before blowing it up—the agent morally ought to expend greater efforts to gather evidence than if the stakes are low—if she is taking a census, for example, then a knock on the door will suffice.[25]

To calculate the evidential probability of some outcome, we must first work out what research the agent ought to do. If she believes her target is more likely to be innocent than her evidence warrants, then her wrongdoing tracks her actual beliefs: she wrongs him more gravely than she would have had her beliefs matched the evidence. If she believes her target is less likely to be liable than her evidence warrants, *and she did not do the requisite research, or responded*

---

[23] We can ask similar questions about whose perspective we should assess these probabilities from. For simplicity, again, I focus on the agent, and each argument works for this approach. But the necessity and endangerment arguments would still be compelling using the victim's probabilities. Developing this point would take me too far afield, but I return to it later.

[24] Pace Michael J. Zimmerman, *Living with Uncertainty: The Moral Significance of Ignorance* (Cambridge: CUP, 2008). On this subject, see also Holly M. Smith, 'The Subjective Moral Duty to Inform Oneself Before Acting', *Ethics*, 125/1 (2014), 11–38. This is not a standard understanding of evidential probability.

[25] Alexander Guerrero, 'Don't Know, Don't Kill: Moral Ignorance, Culpability, and Caution', *Philosophical Studies*, 86/1 (2007), 59–97.

inappropriately to it, then she has acted *negligently*, and thus wronged the victim.

The arguments that support this conclusion are those that underpin *Risky Killing*, though to avoid repetition I will keep them short. First, the agent's negligent act is more disrespectful—her failure to carry out research appropriate to the stakes reflects inadequate regard for the victim. Her negligence also results in her imposing unnecessary risks, since she could have avoided them by doing proper research. Lastly, by proceeding negligently she exposes her victim to unchosen risks of wrongful harm—both the risks that derive from her negligence and the risks relative to the evidential probability that her act will wrongfully harm the victim.

I now have the materials I need for this argument for *Moral Distinction*. The following normative thesis expands on the formulation already given:

Risky Killing: If A kills two innocent people, B and C, and B was more likely, on A's evidence, to be innocent than C was, then (other things equal) killing B is objectively worse than killing C just in case: either A believed B more likely to be liable than C, or, if she did not, that was because of her negligence.

Before turning to war, let me briefly rebut a general objection to this thesis. Could Bruce's likelihood of innocence depend on Aggie's moral beliefs? If she were an act-consequentialist, for example, who thinks rights and liability do not exist, then she would think Bruce is equally unlikely to be liable in both *Sniper-High* and *Sniper-Low*. We might also deny that she *disrespects* Bruce if she maximizes expected value.[26]

I reject this approach to moral justification. If the agent's moral beliefs affected the fact-relative permissibility of her actions, then she could weaken morality's demands just by adopting permissive moral beliefs. This is an unacceptable kind of subjectivism (I will return to this point).

---

[26] I owe this objection to a reviewer for *Ethics*.

Moreover, each of my arguments invokes harms that are *in fact* wrongful. The agent's moral beliefs are beside the point. When Aggie kills Bruce in *Sniper-High*, she is more disrespectful than in *Sniper-Low*, because she reveals herself readier to sacrifice an innocent person for an end that he is not *in fact* required to share. She further aggravates her violation of Bruce-High's right to life by imposing an unnecessary risk of *in fact* wrongful harm on him, whatever her moral beliefs. And for endangerment: our lives go better if others do not subject us to unchosen risks of suffering *in fact* wrongful harms. Although I obviously care about avoiding harms in general, I do not have a special interest in avoiding risks of harms that someone else mistakenly believes to be wrongful.

3. Risky Killing in War

I now argue from *Risky Killing* to *Moral Distinction*. This is only one strand in a pluralist defence of this principle, and does not cover all cases. But it has significant virtues: it is consistent with many combatants and noncombatants being equally (non)responsible for unjustified threats; and it applies to all sides in a conflict. Moreover, these improvements come cheap: I need show only that civilians are more likely to be innocent than soldiers in war, on which I think most philosophers, and most other people besides, would agree.[27]

I argue as follows: first, if one knows about two people only that one is an enemy civilian, the other an enemy soldier, then the former is more likely to be innocent than the latter. Second, combatants in war *should know* whether their victims are civilians or soldiers. If they cannot find this out through reasonable research, they ought not to use lethal force at all (with some exceptions). Third, none of their other evidence overturns that initial assessment. Together with *Risky Killing*, this shows that killing innocent civilians is worse than killing

---

[27] E.g. Cécile Fabre, *Cosmopolitan War* (Oxford: OUP, 2012), 76–8; Jeff McMahan, *Killing in War* (Oxford: OUP, 2009), ch. 5.

innocent soldiers; to get to *Moral Distinction*, we need simply argue that almost all civilians are innocent in war.

Recall that innocence is the opposite of liability. N is liable to be killed if killing her is a necessary and proportionate means to avert an unjustified threat T, and if N is sufficiently responsible for T. N's responsibility for T divides into two parts: her causal contribution, and her agential involvement.[28] If N is the unmediated, necessary, and sufficient cause of T, then she is more causally responsible than if she contributes indirectly, in a manner insufficient and unnecessary for the threat to occur. If N malevolently intends her victim's death, knowing it unjustified, her agential involvement is greater than if it was barely foreseeable that her act would bring about T.

How much responsibility do we need for liability to be killed?[29] Some think the degree varies with the stakes: if killing can achieve more good, then less responsibility suffices. Others favour a context-ually invariant threshold. This difference does not matter here, since we can hold the stakes constant. For now, we can rule out two unacceptable extremes: mere causal contribution, however slight, cannot ground liability; nor is it plausible that only culpable, direct, necessary, and sufficient causes can be liable.

With these conceptual points in place, I can state the argument's first premise:

1. If all an attacking combatant A knows about two potential enemy victims N and C is that N is a noncombatant and C a combatant, then it is more likely that N is innocent than that C is.

The reasoning behind 1 is simple: that N is a noncombatant, C a combatant, tells A that C is more likely than N to causally contribute to unjustified threats. It tells A little, however, about which is more likely to be culpable for those contributions.

---

[28] Recall that one's causal contribution can come about through omission as well as through action.

[29] Introducing here the idea of two thresholds of responsibility for liability, defended in the previous chapter, would both add unneeded complexity and make the argument more parochial than it is intended to be.

To forestall confusion, this premise is consistent with thinking that many noncombatants are at least as causally responsible as many combatants for contributing to unjustified threats in war (as per Chapter 1). Many combatants contribute little if at all; many noncombatants contribute somewhat, some a great deal. But despite this overlap, civilians in general are less likely to contribute to unjustified threats in war than are soldiers.

Some civilians, such as political leaders, financiers, and influential media figures, contribute significantly to unjustified threats, and may count among the exceptions written into *Moral Distinction*, unless covered by some other argument in its favour. But most civilians contribute only through marginal and attenuated financial, political, and moral support. Moreover, those who do not pay taxes, vote, or otherwise influence public opinion do not contribute in even these ways. And of course children barely contribute at all.

Many soldiers contribute no more than most civilians to unjustified threats. But many others contribute just like civilians—they vote, pay taxes, and so on—and also actively participate in conflict. After all, *somebody* does the killing. Many others contribute to the collective effort that results in death and destruction. Indeed, if a member of the military does not at least have a role that contributes to its ability to pose threats, then what is the point of that role? If noncombatants were as likely to contribute to threats as combatants, we would not have a functioning military.

However, soldiers' greater likelihood of contributing to threats does not justify (1) on its own. If civilians were more likely to be culpable than soldiers, that might outweigh their different causal contributions. An agent's culpability for an unjustified threat depends on at least (a) whether she intended the threat, (b) whether she could foresee that she would contribute to it and that it would be unjustified, and (c) whether she had reasonable alternatives to acting that way. However, if A's knowledge that N is a noncombatant, C a combatant, gives her *any* evidence pertaining to these facts, it suggests C is more likely to be culpable than N. Consider each in turn.

(a) C's participation typically involves taking more steps to be part of the war as a whole. This suggests that it is closer to her intentions than for N.

(b) C could more easily foresee that her acts would lead to unjustified threats than could N, since the typical combatant contributes more than the typical noncombatant. Moreover, neither C nor N is more likely to know if those threats are justified. Combatants might sometimes have more first-hand information, but noncombatants have more time to inform themselves and are less indoctrinated. If they are epistemic peers, and C is more likely to contribute causally, then C is taking a bigger risk than is N, which again means she is more likely to be acting culpably.

(c) Lastly, it is hard to say in general whether combatants and noncombatants have reasonable alternatives to making their particular contributions. Conscripts might not, but any country that strictly penalizes conscientious objectors probably also penalizes its citizens for not doing their part. Volunteer combatants, of course, do have reasonable alternatives to fighting.

In summary: C's combatant status is evidence that he is more likely to contribute to unjustified threats than N, and that he is perhaps more likely than N to be culpable for those contributions. (1) follows: N is more likely to be innocent than C.

One might object that, if both C and N are on the just side in a war, A might lack grounds to believe C sufficiently responsible for *unjustified threats*, even if he is more dangerous in general. This would be a mistake. Even if their side is in fact fighting justly, there is always a significant probability that the threats they contribute to are unjustified. Even the best wars involve numerous unjustified threats (including some war crimes), and in realistic cases, we are never certain that we are fighting a just war. As long as this is true, it remains more likely that C contributes to unjustified threats than that N does.

One might further object that (1) applies only to actual cases. We can imagine counterexamples: suppose the noncombatant population includes only adults in a direct democracy who have unanimously voted to launch an unjust war, knowing their decision's ramifications, with no penalties for non-compliance; suppose their armed forces are non-citizen slaves who would be killed if they disobey orders.[30] Then (1) would be false. However, neither this premise, nor *Moral Distinction*, is an exceptionless statement of necessary truths. It suffices for my purposes if it is contingently true in the world as it is.

Premise (1) would be irrelevant to *Moral Distinction* if A could not find out whether her potential victims are combatants or noncombatants. To address this possibility, I need to argue for:

2. Either A's evidence bears on whether her potential victims are combatants or noncombatants or she probably ought not to use lethal force at all.

The First Additional Protocol to the Geneva Conventions requires combatants to bear arms openly, wear uniforms, and separate themselves from the noncombatant population. It gives special legal privileges to those who fight in this way, including the permission to use force and the rights of prisoners of war. In regular conflicts, when combatants fight according to international law, telling them from noncombatants should be easy.

However, *Moral Distinction* applies also in irregular conflicts, in which concealing soldiers among civilians can be necessary to military success. Of course, A can still tell whether her target is actually fighting, which is sufficient for combatant status. But it is a cliché about such conflicts that telling civilians and soldiers apart is very difficult.

For my argument to work, A need only believe that N is more likely than C to be a noncombatant (that is what I mean by A's evidence bearing on whether her victims are combatants or noncombatants). If she does the morally required research, she will at least be able to reach this conclusion. If not, she typically should not fight at all.[31] The

---

[30] For a similar example, see McMahan, *Killing in War*, 217.
[31] See article 57 of the First Additional Protocol, on Precautions in Attack.

stakes could not be higher, so she must bear heavy costs to discover whom she is killing. If she still cannot find out whether her victims are combatants or noncombatants, then she lacks any evidence pertaining to liability, since from any other relevant evidence she could infer her victim's civilian/military status.

Killing someone when you have no idea whether she is liable or not is as seriously wrongful as killing someone whom you know to be innocent. If you are ready to proceed without knowing whether your target is liable, you display your indifference to her moral standing just as egregiously as if you knew for sure that she was innocent. For example, the indiscriminate 'harassment and interdiction' artillery campaigns used by the Russian Army in the second Chechen War were as morally objectionable as the US attempt to bomb North Vietnam 'back to the Stone Age' in the 1960s.[32] Selecting targets at random is as bad as intentionally aiming at the innocent. If A cannot find out whether her victims are combatants or noncombatants, she typically ought to withhold fire.

However, sometimes killing those you know to be innocent is permissible, either as an unintended side-effect or as an intended lesser evil. As presently stated, *Risky Killing* does not apply when: A lacks any evidence about N's and C's status; she has no beliefs on the matter; and she would be justified in killing them even if she knew they were innocent. I think these cases will be very rare, but they are nonetheless exceptions. However, a natural extension of *Risky Killing* would cover them.

The necessity and endangerment arguments work with the victim's probabilities, as well as the agent's. If A subjects N to an unnecessary risk of harm, *on N's evidence*, then that aggravates A's violation of N's right to life; by exposing N to this unchosen risk of wrongful harm, *on N's evidence*, A further undermines her interest in security. Now, even if A does not know whether N or C is a noncombatant, *they* obviously do know. And from their perspective, N is also more probably innocent than C is. The arguments adduced above are

[32] Jason Lyall, 'Does Indiscriminate Violence Incite Insurgent Attacks? Evidence from Chechnya', *Journal of Conflict Resolution*, 53/3 (2009), 331–62.

equally relevant here. They will both be uncertain whether they have contributed to threats, and doubly doubtful whether those threats are justified. With rare exceptions, N should be more confident that she is innocent than should C.

Combatants should find out whether their potential victims are civilians or soldiers. They should bear considerable costs to gather that information. If they have borne all reasonable costs, and still have no relevant evidence, then they ought not to use lethal force unless the stakes are very high. Killing people without regard to whether they are innocent is as seriously wrongful as killing them knowing they are innocent. Cases in which A is ignorant about N's and C's status, but killing is nonetheless permissible, are exceptions to the present argument for *Moral Distinction* from *Risky Killing*, and I set them aside in what follows. Still, a modified version of *Risky Killing* could encompass them, since if both N and C are innocent, killing N is worse than killing C because, *on their evidence*, N is more likely to be innocent than C.

Premises (1) and (2) would not support *Moral Distinction* if A had further evidence, which showed that C was at least as likely to be innocent as N, contradicting premise (1). We need a further premise:

3. In all but rare exceptional cases, the rest of A's evidence is consistent with the probability distribution in (1).

If merely being a taxpayer and voter in a democracy is sufficient for liability, for example, then (3) could be false, because A knows that N is an adult citizen of a democracy. Of course, some adult citizens do not pay taxes, or do not vote, or vote against the government that fought the war. And even if N is probably liable, it is still *more* likely that C is liable, since everything true of N is normally also true of C (as an adult, perhaps a voter, almost certainly a taxpayer), but combatants also contribute in other ways.

Nonetheless, endorsing this kind of low threshold of responsibility for liability clearly weakens *Moral Distinction*. I think this is good reason to reject the low threshold which, as I suggested in Chapter 1, is far too permissive. In lethal self-defence, it is very likely that someone will die or suffer some other severe harm. Either Defender must kill Target or else bear the cost herself. There is a strong presumption against killing Target to save herself, for two reasons. Target has moral status, which prohibits sacrificing him for an equally good, or marginally better, outcome. And it is worse to kill another person than to let oneself die. Defender may kill Target only if there is a moral asymmetry between them that can overcome this presumption.[33] Only a high degree of responsibility delivers this asymmetry; only if the target is significantly responsible is there a proper fit between what he has done and the severity of his fate.

A high threshold might look like the following: some degree of causal contribution and some degree of agential involvement are necessary but not sufficient for liability to be killed; additionally, at least one of those elements must be relevantly *substantial*. A substantial causal contribution might mean being a necessary, sufficient, direct cause. Together with minimal agential involvement, that might suffice for liability to be killed. Substantial agential involvement might mean culpability, which with a relatively slight causal contribution might also suffice for liability.

On a high-threshold conception of liability like this, (3) will be true. In both regular and irregular warfare, very few noncombatants are sufficiently causally responsible for unjustified threats to be liable for that reason alone, and we normally cannot know how culpable they are. War is not the place to attribute guilt, which is difficult enough even in court. Attacking combatants typically target co-ordinates, not individuals; even when individuals are in their sights, they are almost invariably anonymous.[34] And they need not forbear from fighting if they cannot determine their victims' guilt—the risk of killing innocent people must be traded against the importance of

---

[33] This point was best made in Jeff McMahan, 'Self-Defense and the Problem of the Innocent Attacker', *Ethics*, 104/2 (1994), 252–90.

[34] Some think that this uncertainty, and inability to discriminate, means that the innocent soldiers killed in war are not killed intentionally, at least not in the way required for killing them to breach a constraint (Jeff McMahan, 'Who is Morally Liable to Be Killed in War?', *Analysis*, 71/3 (2011), 544–59. I do not take a position on that debate here.

fighting just wars. If we had to find out our targets' culpability before killing them, we would have to be pacifists.

(3) holds true unless A discovers that N is causally responsible enough to be liable even if she is not culpable—perhaps she is a financier who has bankrolled the conflict, for example. Some other argument for *Moral Distinction* might still apply, but if not, this might be an exception. These exceptions will be rare, because so few noncombatants are causally responsible to the required degree.

What if the attacking combatant knows that his targets are politicians? Or munitions workers? Or other suppliers to the military? In both international law and our pre-theoretical judgements, these are borderline cases. In my view, international law protects politicians because of their crucial role in establishing peace after conflict—not on principled grounds. People who are part of the command structure of the military are (morally) combatants.

Munitions workers and other suppliers are harder.[35] On the high-threshold view, they do not causally contribute enough to unjustified threats to be liable unless they are also substantially culpable. Since we cannot know whether they are culpable, they are rightly considered noncombatants. Finding out that N is a munitions worker should not make her less likely to be innocent than C. To see this, consider a simple case. Albert runs the only gun store in town, and sells Ben a weapon. Ben uses that gun to threaten Carrie's life. She can save herself only by killing Albert. I think doing so would be wrong, unless Albert was culpable for supplying Ben that weapon—either because selling guns in general is wrong or because selling to Ben was wrong. Munitions workers and other suppliers contribute less to unjustified threats than does Albert. And mere participation in weapons manufacture is not obviously wrong; otherwise how could we fight just wars? Since the circumstances of war make attributing culpability so difficult, we should think of munitions workers as noncombatants.

---

[35] Cécile Fabre, 'Guns, Food, and Liability to Attack in War', *Ethics*, 120/1 (2009), 36–63.

One might object like this: suppose N is a munitions worker; what if her side is clearly in the wrong, so that she must know that she will contribute only to unjustified threats? Wouldn't she be culpable enough then? In response: first, these general grounds for thinking N culpable will apply also to C, so the additional evidence will wash out, and N will still be more likely to be innocent than C. Second, even conflicts that seem clear-cut with hindsight were, at the time, deeply contested, with radical evidential defects. Hypothetical cases can be misleading. The reality of warfare is always much messier than any case we can describe in a philosophy paper, and there are always reasonable people with diametrically opposed interpretations of the facts.

One might further object that (3) is false in irregular conflicts: suppose A finds out that N has hidden enemy combatants in her house, for example. Should A then reject (1)? I think not. Evidence like this might narrow the gap between N and C, but still, N is more likely than C to be innocent. Although civilians contribute more to threats in irregular than in regular wars, *so do combatants.*[36] Over the last several decades, conventional militaries have been 'civilianized', so that many members of the armed forces have only an attenuated connection to combat.[37] Guerrilla forces do not enjoy the same specialist division of labour. The average guerrilla causally contributes more than the average combatant in regular armed forces. Thus even if N is more likely to be liable in irregular conflicts, *so is C*, and (3) remains true.

Indeed, this point about civilianization of the military can be taken still further. If conventional militaries have clearly distinguished groups that contribute only insignificantly and marginally to unjustified threats, and are not distributed among the rest of the corps, so that on a high threshold they are surely innocent, then the argument

---

[36] On this point, see Benjamin A. Valentino, *Final Solutions: Mass Killing and Genocide in the Twentieth Century* (Ithaca, NY: Cornell University Press, 2004), ch. 6.

[37] Gabriella Blum, 'The Dispensable Lives of Soldiers', *Journal of Legal Analysis*, 2/1 (2010), 115–70.

from *Risky Killing* does not pick them up. Perhaps one of the other arguments for *Moral Distinction* might step in, or perhaps we should consider them legitimate exceptions, like prisoners of war or wounded combatants rendered *hors de combat*.

The next premise applies *Risky Killing*.

4. [From *Risky Killing*]: if both N and C are innocent, then killing N is worse than killing C if either (i) A believes N more likely to be innocent than C or (ii) A believes N no more likely to be innocent than C, because of A's own negligence.

A's negligence is either her failure to gather and respond adequately to the evidence or her decision to proceed, despite the evidence not supporting any conclusion as to her victims' status. Negligent killing is worse when the negligence is more causally significant to the outcome. N has stronger grounds for complaint than C, because A's doing the proper research would have given her more reason not to kill N, but no less reason to kill C. Had she found out that N was a noncombatant, she would have had more reason to spare her; but finding out that C was a combatant would have the opposite result. C cannot complain, then, about A's lack of research, whereas N has definitely been made worse off by it.

We can now make the implications of (1), (2), and (3) clear. Following (1), if A believes that N is a noncombatant, C a combatant, then N is more likely to be innocent than is C. Following (2), on A's evidence either N is a noncombatant and C a combatant, or else A typically ought to refrain from using lethal force. Following (3), A has no further evidence pertaining to N's and C's liability that is more informative than their noncombatant and combatant status. So the probability assignment made in (1) stands up: on A's evidence, N is more likely to be innocent than C. Taking these three together, if A kills N and C, there are four possible scenarios: (a) A's evidence shows that the probability that N is innocent is greater than that C is, and A's beliefs align with the evidence: she believes N more likely to be innocent than C; (b) A's evidence shows that N is more likely to be innocent than C, but A believes C at least as likely to be innocent as

N because she failed to do the proper research or to reason adequately; (c) A's evidence is inconclusive about N's and C's combatant or noncombatant status, and A ought not to use lethal force at all; (d) A's evidence is inconclusive, but using lethal force would be permissible even if both N and C were noncombatants.

In scenario (a), killing N is worse than killing C according to the first disjunct of *Risky Killing* (premise 4(i)). In scenarios (b) and (c), A kills N and C negligently, by proceeding without doing adequate research, or proceeding when she should have held fire until doing more research became possible. Killing N is worse than killing C under the second disjunct of *Risky Killing* (premise 4(ii)). Scenario (d) is an exception to this argument, but is picked up by the amendment suggested above. We can bring these points together into the following premise, and the main conclusion of the argument from *Risky Killing*:

5. [From (1), (2), and (3)]: either A believes N more likely to be innocent than C or, if she doesn't, then with rare exceptions that is because of A's negligence.

6. [From (4) and (5)]: if N and C are in fact innocent, then, with rare exceptions, killing N is worse than killing C.

In other words, killing innocent noncombatants is worse than killing innocent combatants. Before proceeding from this preliminary conclusion to the justification of *Moral Distinction*, one might revive here the 'moral beliefs' objection to *Risky Killing*. Suppose A believes there is no such thing as rights or liability. Or that international law exhausts the moral rules applicable to war. Or she affirms a low threshold of liability to be killed. Each of these moral beliefs would affect the probability that she will kill a non-liable person. She might then reject (1) non-negligently, so (5) might be false.

Suppose that you were unpersuaded by my earlier response to this worry. Two more should help: first, given that the legal corollaries of *Moral Distinction* are so widely endorsed, I doubt whether *anyone* believes that enemy noncombatants are as likely to be liable to be killed as enemy combatants. Second, if A assigns no probability to high-threshold views of liability at all, then she is negligently over-confident in her moral beliefs. But if she assigns any probability to a high threshold, then (5) is true, since it is true on the high-threshold view, and not contradicted by the alternatives. If liability is chimerical, then obviously N and C are equally unlikely to be liable. On a low threshold, *perhaps* N and C are equally likely to be liable, but more plausibly C is more likely to be liable than N. Since C is more likely to be liable than N on the high-threshold view, however A splits her credence between these possibilities (no liability, high threshold, low threshold), the net result is that C is more likely to be liable than N.

We can now defend *Moral Distinction*. It will help to recall the premises so far:

1. If all an attacking combatant A knows about two potential enemy victims N and C is that N is a noncombatant and C a combatant, then it is more likely that N is innocent than that C is.

2. Either A's evidence bears on whether her potential victims are combatants or noncombatants or she probably ought not to use lethal force at all.

3. In all but rare exceptional cases, the rest of A's evidence is consistent with the probability distribution in (1).

4. [From *Risky Killing*]: if both N and C are innocent, then killing N is worse than killing C if either (i) A believes N more likely to be innocent than C or (ii) A believes N no more likely to be innocent than C, because of A's own negligence.

5. [From (1), (2), and (3)]: either A believes N more likely to be innocent than C or, if she doesn't, then with rare exceptions that is because of A's negligence.

6. [From (4) and (5)]: if N and C are in fact innocent, then, with rare exceptions, killing N is worse than killing C.

This gives us all we need to support *Moral Distinction*, at least for innocent combatants and noncombatants. Since, on a high-threshold view, almost all noncombatants will be innocent, we can reach *Moral*

Distinction by arguing that killing civilians is worse than killing soldiers, either because the civilians are innocent but the soldiers are not, or because killing innocent civilians is worse than killing innocent soldiers. Like the argument from opportunistic agency, the argument from risky killing does not work well with a low threshold of responsibility for liability.

4. Conclusion

The argument from necessity helps explain why killing civilians is sometimes so egregiously wrong. The argument from opportunistic agency gives a general reason to think all intentional killing of civilians in war, whether by the just or the unjust side, is worse than intentionally killing soldiers, provided the civilians are not liable to being opportunistically killed. The argument from risky killing is more general still. It gives reasons why killing civilians in war, whether intentionally or not, is worse than killing soldiers, because it involves taking a greater risk of violating their rights to life. When the civilians you kill are in fact innocent, the greater probability when you acted that they would be innocent aggravates the wrong you have done them. This is true irrespective of whether your goals are just or unjust.

Additionally, the argument from risky killing can bolster the argument from necessity, allowing it to extend to the unjust as well as the just side. The central point is this: just as it is worse to kill an innocent person through action that runs a greater risk of violating her right to life, it is also worse to kill an innocent person through action that runs a greater risk of killing her pointlessly. The greater the risk that you will kill an innocent person pointlessly, the readier you show yourself to kill your victim to no end, which aggravates the wrong done to her when you in fact violate her right to life. Killing civilians is worse than killing soldiers even for unjust combatants, because the risk that killing the civilians will be pointless is greater than the risk that killing the combatants will be so.

5

Vulnerability and Defencelessness

1. Introduction

In ordinary thinking about the morality of war, civilians' innocence is the property most commonly invoked to condemn their victimization. But the appeal to defencelessness comes a close second. When Al-Shabab militants occupied a shopping centre in Nairobi, killing scores, UN Secretary General Ban Ki-Moon condemned the terrorists for their premeditated attack on defenceless civilians.[1] The prosecutor of Ajmal Kasab, one of the gunmen in the 2008 Mumbai attacks, highlighted how he had mercilessly butchered defenceless civilians.[2] International criticism of Israel's wars in Gaza, the US and its allies' wars in Iraq and Afghanistan, Gaddafi's repression in Libya, and Assad's in Syria all invoke the same trope. Indeed, I suspect that for any conflict, you can find someone who has accused either side of the special crime of killing defenceless civilians (try Googling 'defenceless civilians' together with the name of any conflict). The idea that killing the defenceless is especially morally wrong is clearly as deeply entrenched in our public culture as is the notion that it is wrong to

[1] UN News Service, 'Ban Strongly Condemns "Totally Reprehensible" Terrorist Act in Nairobi' (2013), <www.un.org/apps/news/story.asp?NewsID=45914#.VHO97Isc-M4>.
[2] NDTV, 'Kasab Gets Death Sentence on 5 Counts, Life on 5 Counts', 6 May 2010, <www.ndtv.com/article/india/kasab-gets-death-sentence-on-5-counts-life-on-5-counts-23619>.

kill the innocent. And yet there is very little philosophical discussion of why defencelessness matters morally.[3]

I think that defencelessness can most fruitfully be understood in terms of vulnerability: one is defenceless to the extent that one is unable to diminish one's vulnerability. There are, then, two kinds of reasons why harming the defenceless is especially objectionable: simply because they are defenceless, and because they are especially vulnerable. In what follows, I first analyse vulnerability and defencelessness, then explain why they matter morally, before considering the significance of these arguments for the ethics of war. Prima facie, it seems likely that killing innocent civilians is worse than killing innocent soldiers because civilians are more vulnerable and defenceless than are soldiers.

2. Analysing Vulnerability and Defencelessness

The first task is to get a tighter grip on vulnerability. Vulnerability is a two-place predicate: a person is vulnerable to a threat. The threat has some prospect of resulting in harm to that person. We can understand this prospect in different ways. One possibility is modal: Annie is vulnerable to a threat if it is possible that she should suffer harm from that threat. This seems far too permissive, however. If vulnerability is to pick out a morally salient property, its scope must be narrower. Better to give a probabilistic analysis.

There are two salient possibilities: the first uses simple, unconditional probabilities; the second conditional probabilities. On the simple account, Annie's vulnerability to a threat is the overall expected harm that she will suffer from that threat. To work this out, we identify all the possible outcomes for Annie that might arise if the threat is fulfilled.

---

[3] Larry May and Henry Shue have developed some ideas along these lines, as has Tamar Meisels, drawing on an earlier draft of this chapter. See Larry May, *War Crimes and Just War* (Cambridge: CUP, 2007); Henry Shue, 'Torture', *Philosophy and Public Affairs*, 7/2 (1978), 129; Tamar Meisels, 'In Defense of the Defenseless: The Morality of the Laws of War', *Political Studies*, 60/4 (2012), 919–35.

We then calculate the expected harm that Annie would suffer in each outcome, by multiplying the harm to Annie by the probability of that outcome coming about. We then sum the products, for all the possible outcomes. For present purposes, assume that we are using epistemic probabilities—the arguments of this chapter do not depend on whether those probabilities are subjective or evidential.

Suppose the threat is that Bruce will mug Annie. To establish how vulnerable Annie is to that threat, we first work out all the possible outcomes for Annie if it occurs. Suppose that if Bruce mugs Annie, he is as likely to just steal her wallet as he is to kill her; but one of those two outcomes will definitely occur. We calculate the expected harm by putting a value on the harm to Annie of being robbed and of being killed, then weighting that by the likelihood that each outcome will transpire. We calculate this by multiplying the probability that the mugging will occur by the probability of this outcome happening if it does. Annie's *simple vulnerability* is a function of the magnitude of that expected harm.

The second possibility is *conditional vulnerability*. On this account, Annie's vulnerability is the expected harm that she would suffer from the threat, *if it occurs*. In other words, we simply calculate the expected harm from the threat, without weighting that for the likelihood that it will actually happen. For example, the McArthur Fire Danger Index, which guides the management of bushfires in Australia, assesses a wide range of environmental variables to determine how dangerous a fire would be, were one to ignite. Strictly speaking, it says nothing about how likely an ignition would be.[4]

In the example above, Annie's vulnerability to the threat is measured by the harm she would be expected to suffer if Bruce mugs her. Now suppose that Bruce might also mug Charles, and that if he does, then he will certainly do no more than steal his wallet. If we hold the probability of being mugged constant, then conditional and simple vulnerability go together: Annie is more vulnerable than Charles in

---

[4] Typically, however, high fire danger days are also days when ignition is other things equal more likely, for example because of lightning.

both senses. But now suppose that Annie is much less likely than Charles to be mugged. Then he might be more vulnerable than she is, in the simple sense, but she would still be more conditionally vulnerable than he is.

Both simple and conditional vulnerability matter morally. Conditional vulnerability is particularly relevant when we cannot predict whether the threat will occur or when it is genuinely open whether it will happen, because it depends on our own voluntary choice. In Australia, about 50 per cent of bushfires are either suspicious or known to be arson, while a further 35 per cent result from accidents.[5] On any given day, it is very hard to predict whether someone will decide to set a fire or accidentally ignite one. Focusing on our conditional vulnerability encourages us to prepare for what would happen if the triggering incident occurs, rather than be distracted trying to predict the unpredictable. And of course if one is deciding whether to pose a threat to Annie's life, then only her conditional vulnerability could be at stake, since it is an open question, within one's control, whether the threat will occur.

Vulnerability is prospective, but it can also be applied retrospectively. Suppose, for example, that in a celebration some guerrillas shoot bullets in the air. Improbably, as they fall back to earth, one hits Annie, killing her. Was Annie vulnerable to the threat posed by the celebrating guerrillas? Her death does not entail much about the expected harm she would suffer. Given the very low epistemic probability that any bullets would fall back towards her, that expected harm would have been very low, so we can plausibly say that Annie was not particularly vulnerable to the threat ex ante.

Annie's vulnerability to a threat is either her expected harm from that threat or her expected harm conditional on the threat occurring. Talk of vulnerability simpliciter is elliptical. It implies some threat or set of threats to which Annie is vulnerable in either the simple or the

[5] Australian Institute of Criminology, 'Proportion of Deliberate Bushfires in Australia', *Bushfire Arson Bulletin*, 51 (2008), <www.aic.gov.au/publications/cur rent%20series/bfab/41-60/bfab051.html>.

conditional sense. Usually the context will determine which threats are being assumed—for example, when we speak about the special vulnerability of children in war, we are considering their vulnerability to threats that are caused by the conflict. In other contexts, we might have special reason for concern about others' vulnerability to threats for which we are ourselves responsible.

Defencelessness is best defined in terms of vulnerability. Annie is defenceless against a threat just in case she can do nothing to reduce her vulnerability to that threat. There are two ways to reduce one's vulnerability: either Annie can act on the threat, by making it less likely to occur or less dangerous if it does occur; or she can act on herself, increasing her resilience against the threat, should it occur. Like vulnerability, defencelessness is scalar. Annie is less defenceless the more she can do to reduce her vulnerability.

Where vulnerability is probabilistic, defencelessness includes an important modal element. What matters is how much Annie *herself* can do to reduce her vulnerability to T. To see this, contrast these cases:

Bodyguard 1: Annie is defended by her hired bodyguard, Charles. If Charles fails to avert the threat, Annie will be killed (and Charles will suffer no loss); if Charles succeeds, then Charles and Annie suffer no loss. There is an 80 per cent probability that Charles succeeds. There is no other way to avert the threat.
Bodyguard 2: The same as *Bodyguard 1*, except that if Charles were not present, then Annie would be able to defend herself with an 80 per cent probability of success.

In *Bodyguard 1*, Charles is defending someone who is defenceless, since Annie cannot herself reduce her vulnerability to the threat. In *Bodyguard 2*, Charles is not defending someone who is defenceless, since Annie could defend herself if Charles were not there. It matters not only that there are measures by which the expected harm to Annie can be reduced, but that Annie should be able to reduce that expected harm herself.

What if your self-defence depends on coordination with others? If that coordination is sufficiently important and pervasive, you might be utterly defenceless on your own, but resilient when together with your confederates. I think it is appropriate to index your defenceless-ness to what you do with others, not what you would do if entirely on your own. The key point is that one is defenceless when one lacks any control over the harm one will suffer if the threat comes about. And while one has less control over collective defence than over one's own self-defence, one nonetheless has some control over the former, and of course it is also much more effective at diminishing your expected harm.

Defencelessness is not the same as conditional vulnerability. I might be wholly defenceless against some threat, but not condition-ally vulnerable to it at all, because, for example, it threatens very little harm. Suppose I am locked into the stocks and you are throwing soft tomatoes at me. I am entirely defenceless, but I am not very condi-tionally vulnerable. Similarly, if I am dependent on someone else for my defence, then I might be not at all conditionally vulnerable—if the threat occurs, my bodyguard will surely save me—and yet still be wholly defenceless myself. A high degree of conditional vulnerability bespeaks general insecurity. Defencelessness is exclusively about my ability to mitigate my own vulnerability.

3. Why Vulnerability and Defencelessness Matter Morally

With these definitions of vulnerability and defencelessness in hand, we can turn to their significance in the ethics of harm. We can immediately see that a victim's vulnerability and defencelessness, if they are morally relevant at all, are relevant only when the victim is not liable to be killed. On most views, liability is instrumental: you can be liable to harm only if harming you will advance some goal. If a liable person is vulnerable or defenceless, that in general means that attacking her will be more effective at reaching the justifying goal. So the defencelessness and vulnerability of the liable is to be welcomed, not regretted. Additionally, when an innocent person is responsible for her own vulnerability or defencelessness, that reduces the impact these properties can have on the moral seriousness of harming her. This does not mean that people who knowingly risk being wrongfully harmed waive their rights against these harms—far from it. Instead it means that your vulnerability or defencelessness are less morally troubling if you could have avoided the threat, but chose not to do so.

Suppose that Charles has killed Annie and Bruce, both of whom were innocent. Suppose that Annie was more vulnerable or more defenceless than Bruce. What reasons would this give us to think killing Annie worse than killing Bruce? I have three arguments that focus on vulnerability and two that focus on defencelessness. The first and third arguments from vulnerability draw from ideas developed in earlier chapters in the book.

I argued in the previous chapter that killing an innocent person is worse the higher the probability, when you acted, that your action would kill an innocent person. The first argument for the moral significance of vulnerability simply notes that if Annie is more vulnerable than Bruce, and they are each equally likely to be innocent, then it was more likely that attacking Annie would kill an innocent person, since it was likelier that Annie would suffer severe harm than that Bruce would. So, for the reasons given in the last chapter, Annie's additional vulnerability entails that killing her is worse than killing Bruce.

To see this, suppose that Charles killed Annie and Bruce using a roulette wheel which was rigged so that, if the ball landed on black 2 (one of the thirty-seven slots), it would detonate an explosive that would kill Bruce, while it would detonate an explosive that would kill Annie if it landed anywhere on black (eighteen of the thirty-seven slots). Charles knew that neither Annie nor Bruce were liable. The ball landed on black 2, detonating both explosives, killing both. Obviously Charles has wronged both Annie and Bruce grievously. But he has shown Annie even more egregious disrespect than he has shown Bruce, and subjected her to a much greater risk of harm, as well as actually killing her. Both acts of killing are unpardonable. But killing Annie was worse than killing Bruce, because, in virtue of her greater vulnerability, it was so much likelier to kill an innocent person.

The second argument starts with an assertion that is near moral bedrock. We have a basic duty to protect the especially vulnerable. When we harm innocent people who are especially vulnerable, we not only breach our duties not to harm them, we also breach our additional duties to protect them. This additional breach adds to our wrongdoing in harming them. Analogously, when a parent harms her child, her wrongdoing is aggravated by her breaching not only her duty not to harm the child, but also her duty of care.

But why should we protect the vulnerable? On the one hand, that question is a bit like asking 'why should we protect the innocent?': we are that close to moral bedrock. But we can say more than this; indeed, there are three promising arguments that we can make.

First, we can appeal to instrumental considerations. Protecting the vulnerable is often a way to do the most good overall: if you can provide the same degree of protection to two people, and one is more vulnerable than the other, then you avert more expected harm by protecting the more vulnerable of the two. However, sometimes the most vulnerable are the hardest to protect, so this cannot be the whole story. Additionally, these instrumental reasons seem not to capture the visceral force of the principle.

The second argument connects vulnerability with the basic principle in moral and political philosophy that we should give greater weight to the interests of those who are worst off. This finds most prominent expression in Rawls's difference principle, and more recently in Derek Parfit's prioritarianism.[6] Rawls argues that primary goods in society should be distributed to the best advantage of the worst off group. Parfit argues that a given amount of well-being matters more, morally speaking, when it is given to someone who is

---

[6] John Rawls, *A Theory of Justice* (Oxford: OUP, 1999); Derek Parfit, 'Equality or Priority', in Matthew Clayton and Andrew Williams (eds), *The Ideal of Equality* (Basingstoke: Palgrave, 2000), 81–125.

absolutely badly off than when it is given to someone who is well off. Suppose we endorse some principle such as this, as a basic datum that moral theory must accommodate. If we should give more weight to the interests of those who are actually worse off now, then we should also give additional weight to the interests of those whom we expect to be worse off in the future. Suppose that Annie will be worse off than Bruce at T_2, so I will have stronger reasons at T_2 to aid Annie than to aid Bruce. If I know at T_1 that this is likely, then I have stronger reasons to aid Annie at T_1 as well, other things equal.

If we have especially weighty reasons to help those who are absolutely badly off, then we also have weighty reasons to prevent them from becoming badly off in the first place. So, if Annie is more vulnerable than Bruce, and other things are equal, then we have stronger reasons to aid Annie than to aid Bruce, because of the greater likelihood that Annie will end up absolutely worse off than Bruce. The 'other things equal' clause is important here. There may be other reasons why Bruce's interests should be given more weight than Annie's; vulnerability generates only *pro tanto* reasons.

The last argument for the basic moral significance of vulnerability draws on the discussion of security in the previous chapter. I defined security as the interest in avoiding unchosen risks of wrongful harm. Vulnerability is a broader concept—it invokes harm generally, not only wrongful harms. But the basic reasons for caring about being secure are the same as the reasons for caring about not being vulnerable. Vulnerability leaves us open to exploitation, makes us anxious, undermines our autonomy, and reflects the fragility of our status with respect to other people. If I am extremely vulnerable, then even if right now I am doing well enough, other people are clearly not robustly disposed to protect my interests across a range of counterfactual scenarios. This too makes me worse off. We have a duty to aid the vulnerable because showing one another the respect that we each deserve as members of the moral community requires that we be robustly disposed to aid one another. If a person is vulnerable, then some of us are not discharging our duties.

The last argument from vulnerability draws on this idea that we are under a duty to protect the vulnerable, together with the discussion of eliminative and opportunistic agency in Chapter 3. Exploiting others' vulnerability for your own advantage is especially wrongful. This is one reason why human trafficking and child abuse, for example, are so paradigmatically bad. The villain is not only harming someone whom they should be protecting, but they're doing so as a means to secure their own advantage. If it is bad to harm someone whom you should be helping, it is even worse to harm them as a means to secure some benefit for yourself. Opportunistic killing is especially wrongful when the victim is especially vulnerable. It is further aggravated, I suspect, when you yourself have created the vulnerability that you are now taking advantage of.

The remaining two arguments apply to defencelessness. I begin by looking at how harming the defenceless disempowers them; then address one more unusual argument, which I think has surprising potential.

If you are defenceless, then you have no power to reduce your vulnerability. This means you are dependent either on luck or on the assistance of others for your avoidance of severe wrongful harm. I have already argued, in Chapter 4, that depending on luck undermines our autonomy, as well as our standing among our peers. But it is also bad to depend too much on others for one's protection against wrongful harm. If you are defenceless, then whether you suffer harm is in the hands of the potential threatener, and your defender if you have one. You are beholden to the whims of others. In Philip Pettit's terminology, you are *dominated* by them.[7] Whether you survive depends on how they are disposed towards you. We have an obligation not to dominate others, and we also have reasons not to contribute to others' domination, by providing the threats that make the potential victim dependent on their defenders. Threatening the defenceless contravenes these reasons.

---

[7] Philip Pettit, *Republicanism: A Theory of Freedom and Government* (Oxford: Clarendon Press, 1997).

When we pose threats against the defencelessness, we deprive them of control over some of their most important interests. We render them dependent on us or on their defenders. This additional harm compounds the wrongfulness of killing them: whenever you kill a defenceless person, you have not merely killed her, but caused her to be dominated and disempowered as well.

Of course, in one sense, whenever you kill another person you disempower him. The difference is that when you kill someone who can defend himself, at least he had some probability of averting this outcome. One might respond: 'if you're dead you're dead, why care about a mere probability of averting the threat?' But probabilities do matter: how well our lives go depends not only on how things actually turn out, but on what could have happened if things had gone differently.

The remaining argument has arguably outmoded origins in the chivalric tradition. When the strong harm the weak, many people intuitively recoil from the fact that it is an *unfair fight*. They think that this alone is enough to account for the special opprobrium that attaches to harming the defenceless.[8]

Of course, it is easy to see why this view is unfashionable. Outside of sport, and other contests in which the competition is an end rather than a means, why should we care whether the fight is fair? Surely we should simply want the otherwise just fighters to win; if they can do so only through fighting unfairly, then so be it. This objection seems right as far as it goes; but it does not totally undermine the fair-fight intuition. Of course we should want the good guys to win, in general. But what if there are good guys on both sides? Or, more precisely,

---

[8] 'To the extent that the distinction between combatants and noncombatants is observed, those who are killed will be those who were directly engaged in trying to kill their killers. The fairness may be perceived to lie in this: that those who are killed had a chance to survive by killing instead. It was kill or be killed for both parties, and each had his or her opportunity to survive. No doubt the opportunities may not have been anywhere near equal—it would be impossible to restrict wars to equally matched opponents. But at least none of the parties to the combat were defenceless.' Shue, 'Torture', 129.

innocent parties on both sides? Then matters are much more ambiguous, and we should want the fight to be at least somewhat fair.

To see this, suppose that among Annie, Bruce, Charles, and Dana none is liable to be killed. Annie, Charles, and Dana can defend themselves, but Bruce is defenceless. If all other things are equal, why should we think that Annie's harming Bruce is more seriously wrongful than Charles's harming Dana, on grounds of fairness? One possibility is that the distribution of risk between Annie and Bruce is more unequal than that between Charles and Dana. Bruce has no capacity to impose any risk on Annie, whereas Dana can impose some risk on Charles. *Pro tanto*, a less equal distribution of risks across the belligerents is more morally objectionable, given that none of them is liable to be killed.

Why should we value an equal distribution of risk? For the same reasons that we care about equality more generally. If all are equally innocent, then each has an equal claim to survive. A scenario in which that is reflected in their prospects for survival is, other things equal, better than one in which it is not. The natural response is to counter that what we really want is for those on the unjust side to bear as much of the risk as possible. We precisely want an unequal distribution of risk. However, in our example none of Annie, Bruce, Charles, and Dana is liable to be killed. Presumably, then, each has an equal claim to survival, so we should regret that their prospects of doing so are unequally distributed, even if all things considered we might prefer that the just cause be realized, despite this inequality.

One might object that if we care about equal distributions of risk, then if Annie could spread the risk of harm to innocent parties more evenly by increasing the total risk of harm, or the risk of harm faced by each person, then she should do so. But this would be a mistake: our reason to favour an equal distribution of risk (like our reason to favour equality more generally) is just one reason among others, and can evidently be outweighed.[9]

---

[9]   Larry S. Temkin, *Inequality* (Oxford: OUP, 1993).

There is more to the fair-fight idea than one might at first think. We have moral reason to prefer a more even distribution of risk of harm across the non-liable, which means preferring a fair fight to an unfair one, when all the parties affected are innocent.

4. Application to War

So, attacking the vulnerable is exploitative, risky, and breaches a basic duty to protect the weak; attacking the defenceless dominates and disempowers them, and generates unfair distributions of risk across the innocent. These, I think, are the best arguments to support the widely shared moral intuition with which we began this chapter. With the major normative premise of the argument in place, the next step is to show that the minor, empirical premise is satisfied. Are innocent civilians more defenceless and vulnerable than innocent soldiers?

It is hard to deny that civilians are more defenceless than soldiers in war. Combatants' abilities to prevent and mitigate threats start with material things. They often have specific equipment that non-combatants lack—obviously weapons, but also protective equipment like gas masks and body armour. They may also be inoculated against some threats, such as biological attack.[10] But these external aids are only the beginning. More important is the training they receive to prepare them for undergoing attack, both as individuals and as a unit. This training engenders both individual and collective aptitude in self-defence. Individual combatants should be psychologically prepared to come under attack—at least more so than a civilian. They should be able to respond to moments of high danger with comparative calm and professionalism. Even if their reason is rendered redundant by pressure and fire, proper procedure should have been drilled into them, enabling them to respond instinctively and to seek cover or fight back where possible. Of course, there will be

---

[10] Kenneth F. McKenzie Jr, 'The Revenge of the Melians: Asymmetric Threats and the Next QDR', *Institute for National Strategic Studies, National Defense University*, 62/1 (2000), 1–104.

individual variations; but my aim in each chapter has been to make a statistical generalization about the relationship between combatants' status and some morally relevant property, not to identify a necessary coextension between them.

Soldiers fight as units, within which each member has a role in securing the others, so that all are safer than they would be on their own. This means not only coordinating to identify and mitigate threats, but also striking back. This capacity, by definition not shared by noncombatants (if they directly participate in hostilities then they become combatants), allows combatants not only to remove the immediate threat, but to deter future ones as well. Equally important is the readiness of combatants to take great risks to protect their comrades. This is in part a normative resource, since combatants often have strong associative duties to protect one another.[11] But much of what combatants do for one another will not be required by duty, but is purely supererogatory. Each looks out for the others; each will take risks to ensure that nobody is left behind.

The point of having armed forces is to equip people to achieve strategic objectives through the use of force; this means making them more effective fighters than they would otherwise be. An integral component of fighting wars is staying alive. If soldiers weren't better able to defend themselves than noncombatants, then the whole purpose of having armed forces would be defeated.

So much for defencelessness. One might object, however, that even if civilians are more defenceless than soldiers, soldiers are in fact more vulnerable. After all, in many conflicts soldiers are much more likely than civilians to be killed. In the sense of vulnerability that uses simple probabilities and looks only at their expected harm, this is clearly right. Although often more civilians die than soldiers, there are many fewer soldiers to start with, so the survival rates are much lower.[12] On the conditional sense of vulnerability, however,

---

[11] Seth Lazar, 'Associative Duties and the Ethics of Killing in War', *Journal of Practical Ethics*, 1/1 (2013), 3–48.

[12] Adam Roberts, 'Lives and Statistics: Are 90% of War Victims Civilians?', *Survival*, 52/3 (2010), 115–36.

things are quite different. For any threat that might occur in war-time, we can be sure that it would affect civilians worse than soldiers if it eventuated. Indeed, this point follows directly from the argument about defencelessness just made: civilians are more conditionally vulnerable than soldiers just because they are so much more defenceless. For any given threat, soldiers will be more likely to survive it because they are better able to defend themselves and one another than are civilians.

Which of these two senses of vulnerability matters more for the ethics of war? Recall that *Moral Distinction* claims that killing civilians is worse than killing soldiers. The operative word there is *killing*. *Moral Distinction* tells us how to evaluate *our* actions. If we are deciding whom to attack, then simple vulnerability is beside the point, because whether or not the threat comes about is still for us to decide. We need to know how vulnerable each potential target would be, if we decide to attack them. We should not ask 'given our current practice of targeting combatants, who is more vulnerable in wartime, combatants or noncombatants?', but instead: 'would combatants or noncombatants be more vulnerable, if we were to target them?'[13] The fact that combatants are likely to suffer more given our typical practice of targeting combatants is irrelevant. Conditional vulnerability is the relevant standard.

Noncombatants are more defenceless than combatants in war and, because of that, are also more vulnerable. They lack the resources and training that combatants use to defend themselves and reduce their vulnerability. If we attack them rather than combatants, then their expected harm would be much greater. The arguments of section 3 show that harming the vulnerable and defenceless is worse, other things equal, than harming those who are less vulnerable and defenceless. Harms inflicted on the vulnerable are riskier, and riskier killings are other things equal worse. Where those victims are not liable, such harms breach an additional duty to protect the vulnerable.

---

[13] And of course we should consider the possibility of mixed strategies, but I set them aside for simplicity.

Moreover they do so as a means of securing the combatants' objective—to coerce the adversary into submission. Killing innocent civilians exploits their vulnerability to achieve military objectives, which is especially wrong. Threatening the defenceless also disempowers them, rendering them dependent either on others or on good luck to avoid severe wrongful harm. It also effects an especially unequal distribution of risk among the innocent. Each of these reasons suggests that killing innocent civilians is worse than killing innocent soldiers.

5. Exceptions and Objections

As with all the arguments for *Moral Distinction* in this book, one can quickly come up with exceptions to this generalization. One might object, for example, that in modern conflicts combatants are routinely subjected to threats that they cannot defend themselves against. This is often true, for example, of aerial or artillery bombardment. If they are innocent, is killing them in these ways as bad as killing innocent civilians? It is not.

First, the same bombardments directed against civilians would be much more destructive, in part because the combatants are only rarely truly defenceless. You can diminish your vulnerability in two ways—either by preventing the threat or by mitigating its consequences. Combatants will typically have means to strike back against bombardment, but even if they do not, they are still trained to defend themselves and to mitigate the threats that they face. And vulnerability in war has more to do with one's vulnerability to the range of threats caused by war than with one's vulnerability to some specific attack.

Second, combatants' vulnerability matters less than that of noncombatants, because, in general, combatants *choose* to make themselves vulnerable, by voluntarily putting themselves in harm's way. If you voluntarily expose yourself to the risk of harm, then your vulnerability gives others weaker reasons for action than if you are vulnerable through no fault or choice of your own, as is typically the case for noncombatants.

Additionally, if enemy combatants genuinely lack either the means to fight back or to escape, then often killing them will be harder to justify than normal. In Iraq in February 1991, the day before hostilities ceased, Iraqi regular forces retreating from Kuwait along Highway 80 were blocked in by the 3rd Marine Aircraft Wing, before being subjected to ten hours of bombardment by US Marine, Air Force, and Navy aircraft. Although many Iraqi soldiers escaped, hundreds were killed in the onslaught. Many people quite reasonably think that what happened on the 'Highway of Death' was morally much more problematic than the regular killing of soldiers in war, undoubtedly in part because the victims were so utterly defenceless. The same moral principles underpin the protections of prisoners of war and wounded soldiers. The outrage (and indeed court martial) that followed the execution of a wounded Afghan insurgent by a British Royal Marine (known only as 'Marine A') is evidence that, when combatants are genuinely defenceless, killing them is much harder to justify.[14] Killing soldiers away from the battlefield, stripped of their equipment and the protection of their comrades, is also often thought distinctly objectionable. Consider, for example, the murder of Lee Rigby, at Woolwich Barracks in London in 2013.[15] This might also explain some of the intuitive opposition that many people have to the USA's use of Unmanned Aerial Vehicles to execute purported militants in the Middle East. In each of these cases, killing combatants is harder to justify than one would otherwise think, and the reason would seem to be that they are distinctly defenceless and vulnerable—indeed, just as much so as are civilians.

Another objection: suppose you are engaged in an unjust attack on ten civilians. Out of concern not to harm the defenceless and vulnerable you first provide them all with weapons so that they can defend

[14] Richard Norton-Taylor and Steven Morris, 'Marine Faces Life Term After Being Found Guilty of "Executing" Afghan Insurgent', *Guardian*, 8 Nov. 2013, <www.theguardian.com/uk-news/2013/nov/08/military-royal-navy>.

[15] BBC News, 'Lee Rigby Murder: Map and Timeline' (2014), <www.bbc.co.uk/news/uk-25298580>.

themselves. Then you kill them all. How did reducing their defence-lessness mitigate your wrongdoing?[16]

First, if you malevolently intend the deaths of the innocent as a means to your ends, that malevolent intention tends to swamp other considerations. It is hard to see any difference between the two cases, because both are so evil. However, once we bracket out that swamp-ing effect, as well as clarifying that your giving the victims weapons does increase their probability of survival, then I see no reason to reject the implications of my arguments here. Although the victims die, they have more control over their own fates when they have the weapons than when they lack them; their probability of dying is lower so the disrespect shown in proceeding is somewhat less; they are less vulnerable so the obligation to help them is slightly weaker; the risks are more evenly distributed (this matters only if the attacker is not liable to be killed). This is not, of course, to trumpet the moral decency of the killer in the second case. What he does is still seriously wrong. But there is *some* difference in the gravity of his wrongdoing in the two cases.

One might pursue a different line of objection, and note that on the foregoing arguments, it is less wrongful to kill innocent noncomba-tants who are well protected by their armed forces, and so less vulnerable than those who are poorly protected; and less wrongful to kill innocent civilians who are well trained at using air-raid shel-ters, and so less defenceless than those who are less well trained. Can this be right?

Given the arguments presented in section 3, this conclusion does indeed follow. If all other things are equal, then it is less seriously wrongful to harm innocent noncombatants who are less vulnerable and less defenceless. However, this does not undermine the argument for *Moral Distinction*—whatever differences there are among non-combatants with respect to vulnerability and defencelessness, they matter much less than the difference between noncombatants as a

---

[16] The example is Jeff McMahan's, and has recently been developed by Jonathan Parry.

class and combatants as a class. Indeed, we can reasonably question just how much protection combatants can actually give noncombatants against lethal attack in war, and how much benefit they can derive from adaptation measures like hiding in air-raid shelters. As we saw in Chapter 2, noncombatants are easy targets; defending them against either concerted attacks or incidental harms is an inordinately difficult job. Even if their armed forces make it a priority, their ability to reduce the expected harm to noncombatants conditional on a set of war-caused threats occurring is limited.

Still, one might press the objection with the following sort of example: suppose you can choose between two courses of action. Setting aside the other salient details, you know that action A will lead to ten innocent deaths, action B to eleven innocent deaths. Suppose you also know that the people killed if you A are less vulnerable than those killed if you B. Supposing everything else between the two cases is the same, ought you to A or to B? Is there some degree of difference of vulnerability for which you ought to B? Or perhaps some number of victims which would allow their lesser vulnerability to justify killing the greater number?

It is natural to think that we should always choose the option that kills fewer innocent people, regardless of their different degrees of vulnerability. Even if this were true, it would not show that vulnerability and defencelessness are morally irrelevant, only that in examples as clear-cut as this we should give lexical priority to minimizing the deaths of innocent people. Where we are uncertain about numbers or where numbers are equal, then vulnerability and defencelessness could still play a role. Indeed, if we know that killing the less vulnerable and defenceless will also lead to fewer innocent casualties overall, then these properties can still strengthen our reasons to prefer killing the less vulnerable and defenceless.

However, this would be the wrong response. Something goes wrong when you kill the especially vulnerable which does not go wrong when you kill those who are less vulnerable—and while examples like this might tend to drown out those considerations, they continue to apply. So, depending on the numbers, even if we know that choosing the course of action that kills the less vulnerable will end up resulting in more innocent deaths overall, we ought to choose it. Of course, in war the point is moot, as tactics that harm combatants are likely to result in fewer innocent deaths than those that harm noncombatants—in part because combatants are more likely to be liable than noncombatants; and in part because just in virtue of their greater vulnerability, a given application of force is likely to kill more noncombatants than combatants.

Ultimately I think that the problem with this counterexample (and with others like it that might be used against my other arguments in this book), is that it invites us to think about civilian deaths in wholly agent-neutral terms. Viewed like this, it might seem that we should simply minimize wrongful deaths. But the considerations at play in this chapter, and this book, are also agent-relative. The ethics of harm is not only concerned with the agent-neutrally optimal distribution of unavoidable harms. By harming others, we are not simply enacting some morally favoured distribution. Becoming a killer is much more morally freighted than this. We have powerful agent-relative reasons to reduce our own involvement in wrongdoing, rather than simply to reduce the overall amount of wrong done. Our reasons to respect rights are agent-relative; so are the properties that exacerbate the wrongfulness of rights-violations. It should therefore be no surprise that sometimes we ought, because of agent-relative considerations, to bring about states of affairs that are agent-neutrally worse than others. This is a familiar and appropriate consequence of accommodating agent-relative reasons in one's ethical theory. It applies just as much to the contrast between eliminative and opportunistic killing, for example—sometimes you ought to kill more innocent people eliminatively, instead of killing fewer innocent people opportunistically.

As long as we believe that some instances of killing innocent people are worse than others, we must sometimes think that we should carry out a larger number of less wrongful killings, rather than fewer more wrongful ones. This might be a reason to reject the whole approach of distinguishing among wrongful killings (and with it the architecture of agent-relative reasons), but as long as we think that approach makes some sense and that we should not simply minimize harm to the innocent, then the same reasoning should also work for vulnerability and defencelessness. Some types of killing are worse than others, and sometimes you ought to minimize your wrongdoing, even when that does not mean minimizing the harm that you inflict.

6. Conclusion

In late 2014, a St Louis Grand Jury refused to indict Darren Wilson, a Missouri police officer who shot and killed Michael Brown, a teenager from Ferguson, Missouri. Black communities across the United States were up in arms, literally, in protest at the killing of this young, unarmed black man. Many factors contributed to the injustice of this killing. Institutionalized racism was undoubtedly at its heart. But it also clearly matters that Brown was unarmed. In part, it matters because it undermines the officer's claim that he believed Brown to be a threat, so exposes the implicit bias behind his decision to use lethal force. But Brown's defencelessness also exacerbated the wrongfulness of his killing. And this is very often true for the killing of civilians in war.

Consider the refugees massacred by the Phalange in Lebanese camps in Sabra and Shatila, or coffee-drinkers in Tel Aviv, obliterated by a suicide bomber, or the guests at the Mukaradeeb wedding massacre in Iraq, killed by US bombing, or the victims of the Lord's Resistance Army in the eastern Democratic Republic of Congo. When you think of all these people and the violent deaths they met, what stands out as making these killings so heinously wrong? Of course, probably all of them were morally innocent—if they were not, then we should not regret their deaths. But many soldiers are also innocent, and yet these killings stand out as much worse than killing soldiers on the battlefield. Moreover, the judgement that these massacres were so egregiously wrong does not seem to depend on working out just how responsible each civilian is. On the contrary, we know at first glance that something very bad has happened here. One way to account for this gut response is that, whatever else can be said about these actions, they involved the killing of many defenceless and vulnerable people. That alone is sufficient to warrant our revulsion, whatever else we subsequently learn.

6

Combatant Non-Immunity

1. Introduction

Throughout this book I have tried to show that killing innocent civilians wrongs them particularly seriously—it is unnecessary, opportunistic, and risky; and they are especially defenceless and vulnerable. Each of those arguments has the corollary that killing innocent soldiers is not so bad. It is often necessary and eliminative, it is less risky than killing civilians, and combatants are not typically as defenceless or as vulnerable as noncombatants are. As much as I have argued for the foundations of noncombatant immunity, I have also sought to explain combatant non-immunity. Indeed, this is perhaps the fundamental challenge for any morally serious just war theory: not merely to explain why it is impermissible to kill civilians, but to do so in a way that allows us to kill enemy combatants. Without an adequate account of this permission, we are inexorably forced towards pacifism. In this chapter, I turn more directly to that task. I consider a series of five arguments, each of which shows that there is something about what combatants do in war that makes killing innocent soldiers less seriously wrongful than it would otherwise be, and so better than killing innocent civilians. Some of these arguments work best for innocent combatants on the just side of a war, some work best for innocent unjust combatants, and some for both.

2. Killing Just Combatants

For the sake of simplicity, let us assume what is false in any realistic war: that all just combatants contribute only to justified threats, if they contribute to any threats at all, so none is liable to be killed. Nonetheless, even if all just combatants are in fact innocent, killing them is not as bad as killing the civilians in whose defence they are fighting, for all the reasons given so far in this book, and for two further reasons, one grounded in a common vice of soldiers, the other in their uncommon virtue.

Most just combatants fight recklessly. This diminishes, without vitiating, their claim to protection against lethal harm. But most just combatants also fight to protect their compatriot civilians. They intentionally draw fire away from the communities that they serve. This, too, lowers their protection against lethal harm, because they offer their opponents a limited waiver of their rights, in return for those opponents concentrating their fire.

On the first argument: in most wars, many just combatants who pose justified threats do so out of sheer luck. Everything within their control could be the same, and yet the threats that they pose could be unjustified, because of the actions of their leaders and others on their side. Members of volunteer standing armies commit to a period of service, knowing the penalties for selective conscientious refusal, without knowing what wars they may be used to fight. Conscripts too fight whatever the cause, to save themselves from the penalties that follow desertion or draft avoidance. Even many warriors of choice, who sign up for a particular conflict, do so recklessly, motivated by the desire to be with their friends, to avoid appearing cowardly, out of jingoistic fervour, or to develop some new skill. Many who sign up for one war end up fighting another. The days of the light brigade might be gone, but still soldiers generally do not reason why: they do, and they die.

Imagine that Annie and her friends are wrongly involved in a bar fight with Bruce and his friends. Annie's crew started the fight, and they know they're in the wrong. Suddenly Charles comes along and, without knowing how the fight started, just weighs in and starts attacking Annie and her friends. As it happens, he is on the right side, and he is effectively helping protect Bruce and his gang. Suppose that Annie can achieve the same defensive effect by harming either

Charles or a random bystander, Dana. She ought simply to stop fighting, and leave everyone alone. But if she does that *right now*, then she is in for a serious kicking. So it is understandable that she acts impermissibly. It is somewhat better for her to harm Charles than to harm Dana, because Charles weighed in so recklessly. Even if he happens to be in the right, he has acted culpably by jumping in, which somewhat mitigates the wrongfulness of harming him.

By going to war recklessly, just combatants who pose threats give unjust combatants grounds for complaint. Moral equals should expect that their fellows respect their rights robustly, not merely by accident. I raised this notion in Chapter 4, when arguing for a right to security. That right is not quite apposite here, since the complaint here is not strictly that just combatants subject unjust combatants to an unchosen risk of wrongful harm—after all, the unjust combatants chose to expose themselves to these risks. Instead, the complaint is simply that just combatants respect their rights by accident.

One might object that, since the unjust combatants are liable to be killed, they are liable to have their rights merely accidentally respected as well. This would be a mistake. The claim that others should respect one's rights robustly (i.e. not accidentally) is not a right like any other, but is itself constitutive of what it means to have rights. Similarly, my claim that others respect my rights in the actual world is not itself a regular right, but is instead part of what it means to have rights. If I have a right to X, then I have a claim that you respect my right to X not only in the actual world, but under various salient counterfactual scenarios. That's just what it means to have a right to X; it isn't an additional set of rights on top.[1]

If you respect my rights only by accident, since everything from your perspective could have been identical, and yet you could have violated my right, then your respect for my rights is compromised. To argue that my claim to respect can be forfeit through wrongdoing is to argue that I can forfeit not just some particular right, but my very

---

[1] Again, the inspiration for this idea is Philip Pettit, *The Robust Demands of the Good* (Oxford: OUP, 2015).

moral status, as a being that is worthy of respect. It is to make me into an outlaw, to whom anything can be done.

The claim that others should respect one's rights robustly is similar to the right to due process, which even the guilty enjoy in criminal court proceedings. You do not forfeit your right to due process by committing a crime, no matter how egregious the crime or how indubitable your guilt. Everyone is entitled to equal treatment before the law, just in virtue of their standing as citizens of a just society. Even when the guilty are punished, they have a right not to be given their just deserts by accident alone.

Of course, these claims can be overridden by other considerations. If you know that a heinous criminal will escape punishment unless you subvert his trial—for example, by doctoring evidence—then it might be a lesser evil to violate his right to due process. Similarly, if your state can fight just wars only by relying on soldiers' willingness to fight recklessly, without regard to whether their targets are liable to be killed or not, then perhaps respecting unjust combatants' rights only by accident is all things considered permissible too. My point is simply that just combatants do something wrong, which just noncombatants do not do, and which helps justify the relatively diminished moral protections that innocent just combatants enjoy compared with their civilian counterparts.

It may also be a matter of luck that any particular civilian happened not to become a combatant. 'There but for the grace of God go I', and all that. But for the just combatants who pose threats, everything within their control could have been *exactly* the same, and yet the threats they pose would have been unjustified. That is not true for any civilians.

The argument from recklessness focuses on a vice of the military; the next focuses on a virtue. The purpose of having armed forces, and the express intention of many who serve in them, is to protect their civilian population from the predations of war. This means both countering threats and drawing fire away from them. Combatants interpose themselves between the enemy and their civilian compatriots, and fight the unjust combatants on their behalf. Their decision to do so constitutes a limited waiver of their right not to be harmed by the unjust combatants, which further diminishes their moral protections against harm.

Obviously, just combatants do not explicitly waive their rights not to be harmed by unjust combatants. However, if they adhere to the laws of war, then they will carry arms openly, wear uniforms, and fight apart from the population.[2] This implicitly invites their opponents to target them, instead of their civilians. Of course, not all armies obey the Geneva Conventions. As already noted in Chapters 2 and 3, sometimes soldiers use civilians as a kind of 'human camouflage'. For these soldiers, the present argument does not apply. I suspect, however, that guerrillas' readiness to expose their compatriot noncombatants to risk diminishes severely their own protections against being harmed, however just their cause.

Just combatants who adhere to the laws of war implicitly say to their adversaries: 'you ought to put down your weapons. But if you are going to fight, then *fight us.*' This alone might be enough to change unjust combatants' moral reasons. But I think that mere implicit consent is not enough: it matters also that what is being consented to is in the consenter's broader interests. Only then is her consent 'morally effective', in the sense of making a difference to other people's moral reasons. Only then does it count as a genuine (albeit limited) waiver of her right against attack.

Most just combatants want to protect their civilians from being harmed in war. All will obviously want their family and friends to be safe; many are animated by a more general civic ideal. Obviously they also have an interest in avoiding harm themselves, but—and this is the virtue in the armed forces—they are often prepared to sacrifice that interest for the sake of others. Indeed, the very fact that they fight

---

[2] On the importance of carrying arms openly and wearing insignia that are visible from a distance, see Article 1 of the 1907 Hague Regulations, and Article 4(A) of the Third Geneva Convention (Adam Roberts and Richard Guelff, *Documents on the Laws of War* (Oxford: OUP, 2000), 73, 245). On the importance of fighting separately from the civilian population, see Article 58 of the First Additional Protocol (Roberts and Guelff, *Documents*, 453).

in accordance with the laws of war is evidence of this, since it involves exposing themselves to risk to protect their compatriots.

Just combatants who obey the laws of war implicitly consent to be attacked; this implicit consent is in their interests; so they effect a limited moral waiver of their rights against attack. The waiver is limited, and conditional: just combatants would of course prefer that unjust combatants not fight at all; but if they are going to fight, then they should target them exclusively. This changes their enemies' reasons. It morally incentivizes attacking soldiers rather than civilians, by diminishing the weight of the reasons against killing the soldiers. Of course, the enemy might not be sensitive to moral reasons at all, but if they are, then this rights-waiver will give them reason to target soldiers rather than civilians, even when they can better advance their cause by attacking the latter.

One might object that waivers of rights elicited through threats are morally ineffective. Just combatants have been forced to fight. Why should their rights-waiver be any different from that of a person who gives up her wallet to a mugger? This objection would trouble me if I was trying to develop a full account of the ethics of war from combatants' consent.[3] But that is not my goal here. I am arguing for a particular and limited waiver. It is particular to a specific conflict, and a specific adversary. And it is limited: just combatants do not grant unjust combatants a right to kill them. They waive their rights conditionally, with a caveat, which makes clear that they are not forfeiting the entirety, or even the bulk, of their complaint against the unjust combatants. This limited rights-waiver is in just combatants' interests, and their natural freedom entails that if they want to waive their rights they should be able to do so. It can therefore be morally effective, and diminishes the protection from harm that they enjoy.

---

[3] For that kind of view, see Yitzhak Benbaji, 'The Moral Power of Soldiers to Undertake the Duty of Obedience', *Ethics*, 122/1 (2011), 43–73. For a version of the objection, see Jeff McMahan, *Killing in War* (Oxford: OUP, 2009); Jeff McMahan, 'Duty, Obedience, Desert, and Proportionality in War: A Response', *Ethics*, 122/1 (2011), 135–67.

One might think that unjust combatants' waiving of their rights to life should not carry the same moral weight. Suppose that confining their attacks to unjust combatants would hinder just combatants' ability to achieve their just cause. Perhaps they need not respect unjust combatants' wishes at that cost. This would be a mistake. The infliction of harm is permissible only if it is necessary. The same is true for the infringement of rights. If killing innocent unjust combatants can achieve the same goal with fewer, or less weighty rights infringements, than killing innocent noncombatants, then the latter would be unnecessary, and so impermissible. If innocent unjust combatants waive some of their own claim not to be harmed, then harming them wrongs them less than it would otherwise do, which justifies shifting more harms towards them, and away from noncombatants. Of course, there are proportionately fewer innocent unjust combatants than there are innocent just combatants, so this argument will be correspondingly less significant for the waiver of unjust combatants' rights against attack, but in principle it still applies.

What of the objection that, even if combatants wear uniform and separate themselves from the civilian population, they might not be doing so voluntarily? Sometimes we can advance a further argument, grounded in collective self-determination. Provided the process by which a community's combatants ended up in that position was reasonably fair, their adversaries have reasons to respect the collectively self-determining decision of that community. It is up to us to decide where the costs of fighting our just wars should fall, and provided we do so in a way that is reasonably fair, then outsiders have the same reason to respect those decisions as they have to respect our decisions about distributive justice, for example, or about the payment of reparations post-war.

I will not try to settle what counts as a fair way to allocate these harms, though there are obviously paradigm cases at either extreme. A volunteer standing army that is staffed by genuine volunteers, who are not forced into that choice by economic circumstance or social pressure, would clearly be fair. Conscription can clearly be fair also, when it is genuinely universal, or based on a fair draft. And obviously filling the armed forces with conscripted members of a despised minority, then sending them off to their deaths, is not fair (as an example, consider the use of the Matabele as cannon fodder by Mugabe in Zimbabwe's interventions into the wars in the DRC, in the 1980s).

Unlike the limited waiver of individual rights by combatants, reasons of collective self-determination do not carry any weight when they hinder the achievement of a just cause. Imagine that an actor wrongly starts a fight; his body, apart from his face, is covered in armour. The actor tells his opponent: 'don't hit me in the face!' His opponent would obviously have little or no reason to respect that request. Similarly, if a political community launches an unjust war, its adversary has little reason to respect that community's self-determining decisions about how the costs of the war should be distributed among its citizens, so unless it costs them little or nothing to respect those reasons, they are clearly not required to heed them.

3. Killing Unjust Combatants

The next arguments presuppose that the innocent combatants are connected to the pursuit of unjust aims, so are primarily relevant to unjust combatants. Of course, in all actual wars many 'just combatants' also contribute to unjust aims, so the arguments could be extended across to them. However, I will not pursue that possibility.

Innocent unjust combatants are members of groups that commit heinous wrongs. They often join these groups voluntarily, knowing the risk that their comrades-in-arms will do terrible things. Some think this alone makes them complicit in their comrades' wrong-doing, and their complicity makes them liable to be killed. On this view, innocent unjust combatants, including those who are not at all responsible for contributing to unjustified threats, can be liable to be killed simply in virtue of being members of a group, other members of which have contributed to unjustified threats that can now be averted by killing the innocent unjust combatants.[4]

To fully develop this proposal, I would need to develop a detailed theory of complicity. But I will not attempt that task, because my reservations about complicitous liability do not depend on those details. Indeed, my central objection is the same as my complaint against any attempt to lower the threshold for liability to be killed, so that people who are not significant contributors to unjustified threats can lose their right to life.

As already argued, there is a strong presumption against killing one person to save another, because the first person is not merely a site for the realization of value, whose interests can be sacrificed just in case doing so realizes a marginally better outcome than letting the other die. To overcome this presumption, there must be a substantial asymmetry between the potential bearers of the impending harm. Subtle, marginal asymmetries will not do. And the mere fact that the target is a member of a group whose other members are responsible for the unjustified threat that one now seeks to avert is not enough to make him liable to be killed. Even if he joined the group culpably, with the intention of doing bad things, that cannot make him liable, any more than his generally bad character can. Suppose that you can save a saint from a threat only by killing a thief; the thief had nothing to do with the threat at all, but he has stolen in the past. The thief's bad character and past crimes are irrelevant to whether he is liable to be killed. He is not connected to this threat, so he cannot be liable to be killed to avert it. The same is true for the mere member of the unjust armed forces. If he is not connected to the threat, then he cannot be liable to be killed.

This point extends beyond talk of liability. Mere membership in a group cannot, on its own, diminish your claim against being harmed at all, unless the group is so evil that you deserve to be harmed simply for voluntarily joining it. Perhaps this is true for a group like the

---

[4] Saba Bazargan, 'Complicitous Liability in War', *Philosophical Studies*, 165/1 (2013), 177–95. See also Cécile Fabre, *Cosmopolitan War* (Oxford: OUP, 2012), 75.

Gestapo, for example. But otherwise, if you do not contribute to the threats that the group poses—if you are a *mere* member—that alone cannot justify harming you.

What if you joined the group knowing that its members might contribute to unjustified threats? Even then, I cannot see why this should make *you* liable to be killed to avert those threats. Perhaps if you had planned to participate, and it was only a matter of luck that prevented you from doing so, that might indicate some negligence or recklessness that could be relevant (as per the arguments above). And again, perhaps if the group is inherently wicked, you might deserve to be harmed simply for joining it. But the armed forces of modern states are not like the Gestapo. Many of them are morally justified institutions—not as good as they could be, no doubt, but still overall justified. You cannot be liable to be killed for joining a morally justified institution, just because you knew, when you joined, that there was a risk that your comrades would end up violating other people's rights.

To see this point, consider an extreme case: volunteer fire-fighting in Australia. Fighting bushfires often involves creating risks to innocent people. Back-burning and hazard-reduction burns can go wrong. Everyone who joins the Rural Fire Service (for example) knows that there is a risk that some of their colleagues will, at some point, make a mistake and cause a threat to an innocent person's life or property. Suppose now that an innocent person can save herself from such a threat only by killing a fire fighter. Perhaps she must push him into the advancing fire in order to escape. It is utterly implausible to suppose that he is liable to be killed by her in this way, just because he voluntarily joined a group whose other members would foreseeably generate risks to innocent people.

Complicity is irrelevant to the ethics of killing in war. You cannot be liable to be harmed defensively unless you have *yourself* done something that contributed to a threat that can be averted by harming you.

In late 2014, the Israeli Government announced plans to bulldoze the homes and revoke the residency rights of the families of Palestinians who carried out murderous attacks in a Jerusalem synagogue.[5] As heinous as those crimes were, the practice of collective punishment is also deeply wrong. Collective liability is no better.

However, while I reject the idea that mere membership of a group whose other members contribute to unjustified threats can make one liable to be killed, I do think that soldiers' membership of the armed forces is relevant to the justification of *Moral Distinction*. Mere membership cannot ground liability. However, members of groups like the armed forces typically have other obligations, in virtue of which it can be better to impose costs on them than on non-members.

Some groups have an institutional structure that allows some members of the group to act on behalf of the group as a whole. By remaining within the group without working to change its decisions, one implies one's consent to being represented in that way. Armed forces have a highly hierarchical structure. They also involve constant positive identification of oneself with the group as a whole, through wearing uniforms. When people in a group's uniform act within the scope allowed them by their role, they represent the group. Soldiers have reasons to take on costs to prevent wrongdoing by their leaders and their comrades-in-arms, because those wrongs will otherwise be done on their behalf. This means that they have a kind of agent-relative reason to intervene. Just as I have a special reason not to become a killer myself, which is weightier than my reason to prevent someone else from killing, I also have a special reason not to allow the group of which I am a part to become a group of killers. The connection to my own agency is undoubtedly looser, and the reason accordingly not as weighty as my reason not to be a killer myself. But the agent-relative dimension to this reason is stronger than if the killing would be done by someone to whom I am wholly unconnected.

We can go further still, and note that when I strongly identify with the group of which I am part, that relationship of representation is

---

[5] See BBC News, 'Israel revokes residency of Jerusalem attacker's widow', (2014), <www.bbc.com/news/world-middle-east-30208693>.

deeper and has greater moral implications for me. This is especially clear within a family: we have particularly strong responsibilities to prevent wrongdoing by those with whom we have loving relationships, partly because we simply want to protect them from wrongdoing and its consequences, but partly also because we identify with them, and think of their actions as representing us in some way. This is particularly so with children. Obviously armies are not like families, and yet there is often a very strong sense of identification among soldiers (especially within units and divisions), indeed one that is cultivated by their trainers and leaders.

And of course group insiders are typically much better placed than outsiders to get their group to change its course. They ought to bear greater costs for that purpose than outsiders simply because they can be expected to get better results if they do so. Soldiers themselves typically have no control over anything besides their own participation. But that is only when they act on their own. When they act together, even a small group can make a big difference. During the Kiel Mutiny, fewer than fifty sailors on board the SMS *Markgraf* precipitated a revolt that ultimately brought down the Kaiser and ended the First World War. What's more, in the midst of conflict, innocent unjust combatants might be able to interdict threats by their comrades. Their proximity to battle affords them opportunities unavailable to civilians (though of course they also face much greater risks—intervening would probably lead to their own deaths).

Of course, all citizens have positive duties to prevent wrongdoing by their state. But soldiers are citizens too. They have all the positive duties civilians have, together with others that derive from their membership in the armed forces. In virtue of these duties, they have to bear greater costs than civilians to prevent their state's wrongdoing. This makes it other things equal better to impose costs on soldiers than on civilians.

Suppose that only you could save a drowning child, but to do it you will have to barge one of two people off a narrow boardwalk. You know that one is the child's father, the other a stranger. Whoever falls off the boardwalk is likely to suffer a serious injury. Clearly, other things equal, you should take the path that barges the father out of the way. One might think that this is simply because the father would obviously consent to being harmed to save his kid. But suppose he is a selfish man, and would prefer his daughter to drown than that he break a leg. Even then, you still should barge him out of the way (perhaps with a little more force than is strictly necessary) rather than the stranger, because the father has stronger duties to save his child, so can be expected to bear more of the cost to that purpose than can a total stranger.

As ever, this argument has limits. Otherwise innocent unjust combatants are probably not liable to be killed just in virtue of breaching their positive duties to prevent wrongdoing by their comrades-in-arms. Their failure to betray their comrades, and sacrifice their own lives, are inadequate grounds for liability to be killed. They have these duties merely because they are members of the armed forces, and as with the argument from complicity, mere membership is not enough to ground liability to be killed (the contrary view would render many more noncombatants liable than is plausible).[6]

4. Killing Just and Unjust Combatants

Combatant non-immunity has two further foundations, each of which applies to both just and unjust combatants. The first is institutional. At present, the laws of war are clear: all combatants are permissible targets in war, and have the right to use lethal force. Civilians, by contrast, are off limits. If the existing laws of war have *any* normative authority at all, then acts that conform to them, even if morally wrong, are somewhat less bad than they would be in the absence of the law.

The law has authority when it can give us reasons for action independent of the reasons we already have. Authority comes in degrees. I have argued elsewhere that international law lacks the degree of authority needed to trump our moral reasons in war.[7] Not

---

[6] Although for an opposing view see Victor Tadros, 'Orwell's Battle with Brittain: Vicarious Liability for Unjust Aggression', *Philosophy and Public Affairs*, 42/1 (2014), 42–77. Steve Woodside's work has also helped me to think through these points.

[7] Seth Lazar, 'Morality and Law of War', in Andrei Marmor (ed.), *Companion to Philosophy of Law* (New York: Routledge, 2012), 364–79.

only are those moral reasons especially weighty, but international law is institutionally underdeveloped. Many doubt whether the law is authoritative even in ideal liberal democracies.[8] And international society is a far cry from an ideal liberal democracy.

However, even if international law cannot supplant our ordinary moral reasons, is it really plausible that it gives *no* reasons at all? Surely not. The law of armed conflict sets a publicly recognized standard which, even if it misses the mark, is better than no standard at all. It does at least solve various coordination problems (how to fight a limited war) and it is an object of agreement in a disputatious world.

Perhaps most important, one might quite sensibly reject the moralistic approach of contemporary just war theory (including this book) as utterly inappropriate to a world containing such a diversity of cultures and moral systems. Following Rawls, liberals often think that imposing on others on the basis of considerations that they can reasonably reject violates a fundamental principle of legitimacy.[9] Instead, we need to find principles for the constitutional essentials—and the laws of war are surely the constitutional essentials of international society—that everyone can agree upon, whatever their overarching moral views.[10] And the laws of armed conflict plausibly form the basis of an overlapping consensus, which most people can endorse from within their own comprehensive system. This gives those laws some authority, so that killing in conformity with the laws of war is somewhat better than killing in violation of them. Indeed, more than just being the object of a hypothetical consensus, the laws of armed conflict are actually agreed to by most states. Of course, there are exceptions, but even states that have not signed up to particular conventions tend to follow them in practice. What is treaty law for some has become customary law for everyone else.

---

[8] E.g. A. John Simmons, *Moral Principles and Political Obligations* (Princeton: Princeton University Press, 1979).

[9] John Rawls, *Political Liberalism* (Chichester: Columbia University Press, 1996), 217.

[10] On this point, thanks to Laura Valentini for discussion.

None of this entails that soldiers ought, or are even permitted, to ignore their moral reasons and obey the law. I deny that international law has *that* kind of authority. But one surely cannot argue that it lacks *any* authority. And if it has some authority, then its permissions and prohibitions affect combatants' moral reasons. And this means that killing innocent soldiers is not as seriously wrongful as killing innocent people in ordinary life, simply because the former is permitted by international law, but the latter is not.

This argument might appear circular: this book aims to vindicate and underpin the law of armed conflict, and here I am appealing to the fact that killing combatants is allowed by the law to justify that law! But my point is simply this: we can imagine a world in which the law of armed conflict were different. And in that world, this argument in favour of the current system would not apply. But as it happens, in the world as it is, we do have this set of laws. And they do affect the moral seriousness of killing combatants. This cannot be an argument for establishing such laws where they do not exist, but it can help to vindicate the thesis that, in the world as it is now, killing innocent soldiers is not the worst kind of killing, which is all I want to show.

The final argument does not presuppose international law. Its central claim is simple: when you voluntarily expose yourself to the risk of wrongful harm, your claim against being killed as a result is somewhat reduced. As ever, it is important to first be clear about what this *does not* mean. It does not mean that you forfeit your right to life by taking a risk. I reject theories of permissible self-defence that construe it as a form of localized distributive justice.[11] Nor do you forfeit your right to security, as discussed in Chapter 4. I also do not mean to invoke the argument made in passing in Chapter 5, that those who voluntarily leave themselves vulnerable and defenceless lack the claim to special protection that their vulnerability and defencelessness would otherwise warrant; I have nothing to add to that argument here. I simply mean that, on a basic

[11] Seth Lazar, 'Responsibility, Risk, and Killing in Self-Defense', *Ethics*, 119/4 (2009), 699–728.

principle of distributive justice, if there are costs that must be distributed, then other things equal it is better that they fall on those whose voluntary actions foreseeably contributed to those costs falling due. Those who are more responsible for the threat arising had more opportunity to avoid it coming about, and it is better that the costs fall on those who had some opportunity to avoid them than on those who did not. Combatants, on either side, choose to act in ways that make it more likely that they will be harmed. Noncombatants do not make those choices. This alone gives us reason to direct threats towards soldiers, and away from civilians.

Of course, if my voluntary choices are just one contributing factor, and others' voluntary and *wrongful* choices were also necessary for this cost to come about, then clearly *compared with them* I am not the appropriate one to bear the harm. But when compared with someone who had no causal involvement at all, then there is somewhat more reason for me to bear the cost than for them to do so. Return to the dangerous neighbourhood. Suppose I am a mugger. I can mug the guy who chose to walk into the dodgy neighbourhood at night or head across town and mug somebody there. Obviously both acts are impermissible. But it is worse to harm the people who have done nothing to expose themselves to risk.

In war, as already noted, just combatants expose themselves to risk to protect their compatriot civilians. It seems harsh that, in virtue of this self-sacrifice, they should wind up being more appropriate objects of lethal force than the people they are trying to protect. But I do not mean to imply criticism of those just combatants. They have not lost any rights by subjecting themselves to risk. They do not deserve to be harmed, nor is it appropriate for unjust combatants to harm them. A basic principle of distributive justice, which says that costs should follow choice, gives more reason to impose costs on innocent combatants than on innocent noncombatants, since the combatants have generally chosen to be involved in the violence, but the noncombatants have not. Given that they have indeed chosen to put themselves at risk precisely to protect their civilian counter-parts, I see nothing incongruous in their being, as a result, more appropriate targets than those they are trying to protect.

5. Conclusion

This book has tried to explain why we shouldn't kill civilians in war. But this, in a sense, should be easy to do. It is justifying killing that is hard. And if pacifism is false—and I assume for the sake of argument that it is—then we must somehow justify the killing that war inevitably involves. And we must do so in a way that does not open the floodgates, embroiling more civilians in the carnage of war than is morally tolerable. This is why, in the canonical text in twentieth-century just war theory, noncombatant immunity and the moral equality of combatants go hand in hand: the source of civilian immunity is the same as the source of combatant liability.[12] I made clear my disagreements with Walzer at the outset. But he was clearly on to something: to explain why it is impermissible to kill civilians in war, we have to say why it is permissible to kill soldiers. Or at least, why killing soldiers—however just their cause—is not as bad as killing an innocent person in ordinary life, outside of war. The arguments of Chapters 2–5 support this thesis. Killing soldiers is often necessary and eliminative, and is less risky than killing civilians, and soldiers are either less vulnerable and defenceless, or else are responsible for their own vulnerability and defencelessness.

This chapter's arguments turn the screw further. Even innocent just combatants take risks by fighting without regard to whether their war is just, which diminishes their moral standing; they voluntarily put themselves in harm's way, trading a limited waiver of their right to life for a greater likelihood that their enemies will target them instead of their civilians; as members of the armed forces that are fighting unjustly, they have greater responsibilities to prevent wrongdoing by their comrades, which give others more reason to impose costs on them than on others who lack those omissive

---

[12] Michael Walzer, *Just and Unjust Wars: A Moral Argument with Historical Illustrations* (New York: Basic Books, 2006).

responsibilities; they fight in accordance with a broadly authoritative international law; and they voluntarily expose themselves to risk. None of these considerations grounds liability to be killed. But they all help explain why killing innocent soldiers is not as bad as killing innocent civilians.

Epilogue
Sparing Civilians

Civilians are almost never liable to be killed. Combatants, especially on the unjust side, sometimes are. This alone explains why killing civilians is often so much worse than killing soldiers. But it is not enough. Many soldiers, especially but not only on the just side, also retain their rights to life. Why is killing innocent civilians worse than killing innocent soldiers? Each of the chapters of this book has sought to answer this question. Each has identified reasons for thinking that killing civilians in war is an especially execrable species of killing the innocent, while killing innocent soldiers is considerably less seriously wrongful than that.

Each argument admits of exceptions. Sometimes killing soldiers is wholly unnecessary; sometimes it is wholly opportunistic; sometimes it is totally obvious that the soldiers are innocent; and sometimes they are wholly vulnerable and defenceless, through no choice of their own. They do not all volunteer to fight, or go to war recklessly. I suspect that almost all combatants intend to draw fire away from their compatriot counterparts, but perhaps there are exceptions to that too. Not all the innocent unjust combatants have additional positive duties to bear costs to prevent their comrades-in-arms' wrongdoing; not all voluntarily expose themselves to risk; and not all fight in accordance with international law. And we could tell the same story in reverse for civilians: each of my arguments has made an empirical generalization which I believe to be true, but which will not hold for every individual.

Moral Distinction has multiple overlapping foundations. If a soldier or civilian falls on the unexpected side of the line for every single one of these, then ultimately the mere fact that he is or is not a combatant is morally inert. Membership of the armed forces matters to your omissive responsibilities, to be sure. But the differences that matter morally are those introduced and defended in this book. These overlap enough with combatant and noncombatant status that killing noncombatants is almost always worse than killing combatants. Any remaining exceptions are genuine, legitimate exceptions to the rule.

Many of these reasons come down to the fact that, in general, combatants but not noncombatants are 'dangerous men'. Soldiers pose threats, civilians do not. Walzer thought this made all soldiers liable to be killed. That was wrong. But the fact that so many soldiers pose threats is relevant to the moral seriousness of killing them, relative to that of killing civilians. Walzer was right about that. That soldiers pose threats makes killing them necessary and eliminative; it supports the view that they are more likely than civilians to be liable to be killed; and it diminishes their vulnerability and defencelessness. This is especially important for just combatants. That they pose threats, when they do, makes killing them somewhat easier to justify, even if it is still impermissible.

Moral Distinction does not get us all the way to the protection of noncombatants in war. For that, we need laws of armed conflict, and in those laws principles such as noncombatant immunity, proportionality, and precautions in attack are the right ones. The arguments for *Moral Distinction* provide a crucial step to explain how we can justify these protections for noncombatants, without having to extend them to combatants as well. Equally important, the arguments show why killing civilians is so absolutely wrongful, so often, which helps to vindicate the visceral outrage that anti-civilian attacks invoke, which is also necessary to buttress support for those laws.

Of course, these results do not come for free: the arguments from necessity, eliminative agency, risk, and vulnerability/defencelessness all worked best on the assumption of a high threshold account of liability to be killed. Justifying *Moral Distinction* on a low threshold account—according to which any degree of responsibility for an unjustified threat can suffice to make one liable to be killed—is a much more challenging task. And even if one could vindicate *Moral Distinction* on a low-threshold view, getting from there to the protection of noncombatants in war would be a challenge, since for that we need to show not only that killing civilians is worse than killing soldiers, but that it is egregiously wrongful. If many civilians are in fact liable to be killed in war, then we cannot endorse that absolute claim. So much the worse, I think, for low-threshold accounts of liability to be killed: their failure to justify the protection of noncombatants in war counts against them.

But there is another way to justify the protection of noncombatants in war, without going into these foundational arguments, to which low-threshold theorists and others might appeal. Instead of knowing it by its roots, we could know it by its fruits: perhaps laws enforcing noncombatant immunity, proportionality, and precautions in attack are justified by their usefulness, over the long run. Perhaps what we really need is a code to limit the suffering and wrongdoing in war, and all of these non-instrumental arguments are just a sideshow.[1]

Although I find this view unpersuasive, it is important to see the truth in it. We do need a code. Beyond moral argument, we do need laws, standards that can be widely promulgated and (relatively) easily applied. And we need to promote respect for existing international law. But we do this better by vindicating it with intrinsic moral justifications, than by arguing that it is a convenient shorthand, a rule of thumb that broadly gives the best results overall. People will be more motivated to obey international law if it tracks our moral reasons than if it is just a useful proxy.

Moreover, we have to give *some* account of the moral reasons that govern armed conflict—clearly we cannot focus on law alone. And if that account does not vindicate *Moral Distinction*, then we will quickly face the question: why should we obey international law when it diverges from our underlying moral reasons? International

---

[1] This view has many advocates, but its importance has most forcefully been pressed on me, separately, by Henry Shue and Philip Pettit.

law lacks the kind of authority that could trump reasons as fundamental as those engaged when killing in war. The duties grounded in our opponents' rights to life cannot be overridden by legal permissions.

If we want people to obey international law, then we should try to vindicate it with non-instrumental moral arguments. And in any case we need an account of our moral reasons in war. If that account lacks a defence of *Moral Distinction*, then current international law diverges so far from war's morality that we should not extol obedience, but should instead press for radical change.

Bibliography

Abrahms, Max (2006), 'Why Terrorism Does Not Work', *International Security*, 31(2), 42–78.

Abrahms, Max (2007), 'Why Democracies Make Superior Counterterrorists', *Security Studies*, 16(2), 223–53.

Abrahms, Max (2008), 'What Terrorists Really Want: Terrorist Motives and Counterterrorism Strategy', *International Security*, 32(4), 78–105.

Arneson, Richard J. (2006), 'Just Warfare Theory and Noncombatant Immunity', *Cornell International Law Journal*, 39, 663–88.

Australian Institute of Criminology (2008), 'Proportion of Deliberate Bushfires in Australia', *Bushfire Arson Bulletin*, 51, <www.aic.gov.au/publications/current%20series/bfab/41-60/bfab051.html>.

Bannerjee, Sikata (2000), *Warriors in Politics: Hindu Nationalism, Violence, and the Shiv Sena in India* (Boulder, Colo.: Westview Press).

Bazargan, Saba (2013), 'Complicitous Liability in War', *Philosophical Studies*, 165(1), 177–95.

Bazargan, Saba (2014), 'Killing Minimally Responsible Threats', *Ethics*, 125(1), 114–36.

BBC News (2014), 'Lee Rigby Murder: Map and Timeline', <www.bbc.co.uk/news/uk-25298580>.

BBC News (2014), 'Israel revokes residency of Jerusalem attacker's widow', <www.bbc.com/news/world-middle-east-30208693>.

Benbaji, Yitzhak (2011), 'The Moral Power of Soldiers to Undertake the Duty of Obedience', *Ethics*, 122(1), 43–73.

bin Laden, Osama (2002), 'Letter to America', *Guardian*, 24 Nov., <www.theguardian.com/world/2002/nov/24/theobserver>.

Bloom, Mia M. (2004), 'Palestinian Suicide Bombing: Public Support, Market Share, and Outbidding', *Political Science Quarterly*, 119(1), 61–88.

Blum, Gabriella (2010), 'The Dispensable Lives of Soldiers', *Journal of Legal Analysis*, 2(1), 115–70.

Briggs, Rachael (2010), 'The Metaphysics of Chance', *Philosophy Compass*, 5(11), 938–52.

Chalk, Peter (1999), 'The Evolving Dynamic of Terrorism in the 1990s', *Australian Journal of International Affairs*, 53(2), 151–68.

Chenowith, Erica (2011), *Why Civil Resistance Works: The Strategic Logic of Nonviolent Conflict* (New York: Columbia University Press).

Christopher, Russell (1998), 'Self-Defense and Defense of Others', *Philosophy and Public Affairs*, 27(2), 123–41.

Coady, Tony (2008), *Morality and Political Violence* (Cambridge: Cambridge University Press).

De Finetti, Bruno (1990), *Theory of Probability: A Critical Introductory Treatment*, 2 vols (Wiley Classics Library edn; Chichester: Wiley).

Dill, Janina, and Shue, Henry (2012), 'Limiting the Killing in War: Military Necessity and the St. Petersburg Assumption', *Ethics and International Affairs*, 26(3), 311–33.

Douhet, Giulio (1983), *The Command of the Air* (USAF Warrior Studies; Washington, DC: Office of Air Force History).

Downes, Alexander (2006), 'Desperate Times, Desperate Measures: The Causes of Civilian Victimization in War', *International Security*, 30(4), 152–95.

Downes, Alexander (2007), 'Draining the Sea by Filling the Graves: Investigating the Effectiveness of Indiscriminate Violence as a Counterinsurgency Strategy', *Civil Wars*, 9(4), 420–44.

Downes, Alexander, and Cochran, Kathryn McNabb (2010), 'Targeting Civilians to Win? Assessing the Military Effectiveness of Civilian Victimization in Interstate War', in Erica Chenowith and Adria Lawrence (eds), *Rethinking Violence: States and Non-State Actors in Conflict* (Cambridge, Mass.: MIT Press), 23–56.

Downes, Alexander, and Cochran, Kathryn McNabb (2011), 'It's a Crime, But is it a Blunder? The Efficacy of Targeting Civilians in War', Unpublished MS.

Eiland, Giora (2014), 'In Gaza, there is No Such Thing as "Innocent Civilians"', *Ynetnews.com*, <www.ynetnews.com/articles/0,7340,L-4554583,00.html>.

Fabre, Cécile (2009), 'Guns, Food, and Liability to Attack in War', *Ethics*, 120(1), 36–63.

Fabre, Cécile (2012), *Cosmopolitan War* (Oxford: Oxford University Press).

Frowe, Helen (2011), 'Self-Defence and the Principle of Non-Combatant Immunity', *Journal of Moral Philosophy*. 8(4), 530–46.

Frowe, Helen (2014), *Defensive Killing* (Oxford: Oxford University Press).

Gans, Chaim (2008), *A Just Zionism* (Oxford: Oxford University Press).

Gartner, Scott Sigmund, and Segura, Gary M. (1998), 'War, Casualties, and Public Opinion', *Journal of Conflict Resolution*, 42(3), 278–300.

Gray, Colin S. (1999), *Modern Strategy* (Oxford: Oxford University Press).

Gross, Michael (2005–6), 'Killing Civilians Intentionally: Double Effect, Reprisal, and Necessity in the Middle East', *Political Science Quarterly*, 120(4), 555–79.

Gross, Michael (2010), *Moral Dilemmas of Modern War: Torture, Assassination and Blackmail in an Age of Asymmetric Conflict* (Cambridge: Cambridge University Press).

Guerrero, Alexander (2007), 'Don't Know, Don't Kill: Moral Ignorance, Culpability, and Caution', *Philosophical Studies*, 86(1), 59–97.

Hansson, Sven Ove (2003), 'Ethical Criteria of Risk Acceptance', *Erkenntnis*, 59(3), 291–309.

Haque, Adil Ahmad (2011), 'Protecting and Respecting Civilians: Correcting the Substantive and Structural Defects of the Rome Statute', *New Criminal Law Review*, 14(4), 519–75.

Haque, Adil Ahmad (2012), 'Killing in the Fog of War', *Southern California Law Review*, 86(1), 63–116.

Harmon, C. C. (2001), 'Five Strategies of Terrorism', *Small Wars and Insurgencies*, 12(3), 39–66.

Hastings, Michael (2010), 'The Runaway General', *Rolling Stone*, 1108/1109 (8–22 July), <www.rollingstone.com/politics/news/the-runaway-general-20100622>.

Hayenhjelm, Madeleine, and Wolff, Jonathan (2012), 'The Moral Problem of Risk Impositions: A Survey', *European Journal of Philosophy*, 20(S1), 26–51.

Holmes, Robert (1989), *On War and Morality* (Princeton: Princeton University Press).

Horowitz, Michael, and Reiter, Dan (2001), 'When does Aerial Bombing Work? Quantitative Empirical Tests, 1917–1999', *Journal of Conflict Resolution*, 45(2), 147–73.

Human Rights Watch (2002), *Erased in a Moment: Suicide Bombing Attacks Against Israeli Civilians* (New York: Human Rights Watch).

John, Stephen (2011), 'Security, Knowledge and Well-Being', *Journal of Moral Philosophy*, 8(1), 68–91.

Kahl, Colin H. (2007), 'In the Crossfire or the Crosshairs? Norms, Civilian Casualties, and U.S. Conduct in Iraq', *International Security*, 32(1), 7–46.

Kahn, Paul W. (2002), 'The Paradox of Riskless Warfare', *Philosophy and Public Policy Quarterly*, 22(3), 2–8.

Kalyvas, Stathis N. (1999), 'Wanton and Senseless? The Logic of Massacres in Algeria', *Rationality and Society*, 11(3), 243–85.

Kalyvas, Stathis N. (2004), 'The Paradox of Terrorism in Civil War', *Journal of Ethics*, 8(1), 97–138.

Kamm, Frances M. (2004), 'Failures of Just War Theory: Terror, Harm, and Justice', *Ethics*, 114(4), 650–92.

Kasher, Asa, and Yadlin, Amos (2005), 'Military Ethics of Fighting Terror: An Israeli Perspective', *Journal of Military Ethics*, 4, 3–32.

Keinon, Herb (2014), 'PM: Terrorists Watching Whether World Gives Immunity for Attacks from Schools, Homes', *Jerusalem Post*, 6 Aug., <www.jpost.

com/Operation-Protective-Edge/WATCH-LIVE-Netanyahu-addresses-foreign-press-in-aftermath-of-Gaza-operation-370255>.

Kocher, Matthew Adam, Pepinsky, Thomas B., and Kalyvas, Stathis N. (2011), 'Aerial Bombing and Counterinsurgency in the Vietnam War', *American Journal of Political Science*, 55(2), 1–18.

Kydd, Andrew H., and Walter, Barbara F. (2006), 'The Strategies of Terrorism', *International Security*, 31(1), 49–79.

Lazar, Seth (2009a), 'The Nature and Disvalue of Injury', *Res Publica*, 15(3), 289–304.

Lazar, Seth (2009b), 'Responsibility, Risk, and Killing in Self-Defense', *Ethics*, 119(4), 699–728.

Lazar, Seth (2010a), 'A Liberal Defence of (Some) Duties to Compatriots', *Journal of Applied Philosophy*, 27(3), 246–57.

Lazar, Seth (2010b), 'The Responsibility Dilemma for *Killing in War:* A Review Essay', *Philosophy and Public Affairs*, 38(2), 180–213.

Lazar, Seth (2012a), 'Morality and Law of War', in Andrei Marmor (ed.), *Companion to Philosophy of Law* (New York: Routledge), 364–79.

Lazar, Seth (2012b), 'Necessity in Self-Defense and War', *Philosophy and Public Affairs*, 40(1), 3–44.

Lazar, Seth (2013), 'Associative Duties and the Ethics of Killing in War', *Journal of Practical Ethics*, 1(1), 3–48.

Lazar, Seth (2014a), 'In Dubious Battle: Uncertainty and the Ethics of Killing', Unpublished MS.

Lazar, Seth (2014b), 'On Human Shields', *Boston Review*, 5 Aug., <http://www.bostonreview.net/world/seth-lazar-human-shields>.

Lenman, James (2008), 'Contractualism and Risk Imposition', *Politics, Philosophy and Economics*, 7(1), 99–122.

Lichtenberg, Judith (1994), 'War, Innocence, and the Doctrine of Double Effect', *Philosophical Studies*, 74 (3), 347–68.

Luban, David (2014), 'Risk Taking and Force Protection', in Yitzhak Benbaji and Naomi Sussman (eds), *Reading Walzer* (New York: Routledge), 230–56.

Lutz, James M., and Lutz, Brenda J. (2009), 'How Successful is Terrorism?', *Forum on Public Policy*, online, 1, 1–22, <http://forumonpublicpolicy.com/spring09papers/archivespr09/lutz.pdf >.

Lyall, Jason (2009), 'Does Indiscriminate Violence Incite Insurgent Attacks? Evidence from Chechnya', *Journal of Conflict Resolution*, 53(3), 331–62.

McKenzie Jr, Kenneth F. (2000), 'The Revenge of the Melians: Asymmetric Threats and the Next QDR', *Institute for National Strategic Studies, National Defense University*, 62(1).

McKeogh, Colm (2002), *Innocent Civilians: The Morality of Killing in War* (Basingstoke: Palgrave).

McMahan, Jeff (1994a), 'Innocence, Self-Defense and Killing in War', *Journal of Political Philosophy*, 2(3), 193–221.

McMahan, Jeff (1994b), 'Self-Defense and the Problem of the Innocent Attacker', *Ethics*, 104(2), 252–90.

McMahan, Jeff (2004), 'The Ethics of Killing in War', *Ethics*, 114(1), 693–732.

McMahan, Jeff (2006), 'Killing in War: A Reply to Walzer', *Philosophia*, 34(1), 47–51.

McMahan, Jeff (2009), *Killing in War* (Uehiro Series in Practical Ethics; Oxford: Oxford University Press).

McMahan, Jeff (2010), 'The Just Distribution of Harm between Combatants and Noncombatants', *Philosophy and Public Affairs*, 38(4), 342–79.

McMahan, Jeff (2011a), 'Who is Morally Liable to Be Killed in War?', *Analysis*, 71(3), 544–59.

McMahan, Jeff (2011b), 'Duty, Obedience, Desert, and Proportionality in War: A Response', *Ethics*, 122(1), 135–67.

McMahan, Jeff (2014), 'What Rights May Be Defended by Means of War?', in Seth Lazar and Cécile Fabre (eds), *The Morality of Defensive War* (Oxford: Oxford University Press), 115–58.

McNaughton, David, and Rawling, Piers (1991), 'Agent-Relativity and the Doing-Happening Distinction', *Philosophical Studies: An International Journal for Philosophy in the Analytic Tradition*, 63(2), 167–85.

McNaughton, David, and Rawling, Piers (1995), 'Value and Agent-Relative Reasons', *Utilitas*, 7(1), 31–47.

McPherson, Lionel (2004), 'Innocence and Responsibility in War', *Canadian Journal of Philosophy*, 34(4), 485–506.

Manu (1991), *The Laws of Manu* (Penguin Classics; London: Penguin).

Mason, David (1996), 'Insurgency, Counterinsurgency, and the Rational Peasant', *Public Choice*, 86(1/2), 63–83.

Mavrodes, George I. (1975), 'Conventions and the Morality of War', *Philosophy and Public Affairs*, 4(2), 117–31.

May, Larry (2007), *War Crimes and Just War* (Cambridge: Cambridge University Press).

Meisels, Tamar (2012), 'In Defense of the Defenseless: The Morality of the Laws of War', *Political Studies*, 60(4), 919–35.

Moghadam, Assaf (2008/2009), 'Motives for Martyrdom: Al-Qaeda, Salafi Jihad, and the Spread of Suicide Attacks', *International Security*, 33(3), 46–78.

Munir, Muhammad (2011), 'The Protection of Civilians in War: Non-Combatant Immunity in Islamic Law War', *Hamdard Islamicus*, 34(4), <http://works.bepress.com/muhammad_munir/13>.

Münkler, Herfried (2002), *The New Wars* (Cambridge: Polity).

Nagel, Thomas (1986), *The View from Nowhere* (Oxford: Oxford University Press).

NDTV (2010), 'Kasab Gets Death Sentence on 5 Counts, Life on 5 Counts', *NDTV. COM*, 6 May, <www.ndtv.com/article/india/kasab-gets-death-sentence-on-5-counts-life-on-5-counts-23619>.

Norman, Richard (1995), *Ethics, Killing and War* (Cambridge: Cambridge University Press).

Norton-Taylor, Richard, and Morris, Steven (2013), 'Marine Faces Life Term After Being Found Guilty of "Executing" Afghan Insurgent', *Guardian*, 8 Nov., <www.theguardian.com/uk-news/2013/nov/08/military-royal-navy>.

Nozick, Robert (1974), *Anarchy, State and Utopia* (Oxford: Basil Blackwell).

Oberdiek, John (2012), 'The Moral Significance of Risking', *Legal Theory*, 18(3), 339–56.

Øverland, Gerhard (2005), 'Killing Civilians', *European Journal of Philosophy*, 13(3), 345–63.

Øverland, Gerhard (2014), 'Moral Obstacles: An Alternative to the Doctrine of Double Effect', *Ethics*, 124(3), 481–506.

Pape, Robert (1996), *Bombing to Win: Air Power and Coercion in War* (London: Cornell University Press).

Pape, Robert (2003), 'The Strategic Logic of Suicide Terrorism', *American Political Science Review*, 97(3), 343–61.

Pape, Robert (2005), *Dying to Win: The Strategic Logic of Suicide Terrorism* (New York: Random House).

Parfit, Derek (1984), *Reasons and Persons* (Oxford: Clarendon Press).

Parfit, Derek (2000), 'Equality or Priority', in Matthew Clayton and Andrew Williams (eds), *The Ideal of Equality* (Basingstoke: Palgrave), 81–125.

Parfit, Derek (2011), *On What Matters* (Oxford: Oxford University Press).

Perry, Stephen (2007), 'Risk, Harm, Interests, and Rights', in Tim Lewens (ed.), *Risk: Philosophical Perspectives* (New York: Routledge), 190–210.

Pettit, Philip (1987), 'Universalizability without Utilitarianism', *Mind*, 96(381), 74–82.

Pettit, Philip (1997), *Republicanism: A Theory of Freedom and Government* (Oxford Political Theory; Oxford: Clarendon Press).

Pettit, Philip (2008), 'Freedom and Probability: A Comment on Goodin and Jackson', *Philosophy and Public Affairs*, 36(2), 206–20.

Pettit, Philip (2015), *The Robust Demands of the Good* (Oxford: Oxford University Press).

Portmore, Douglas W. (2001), 'McNaughton and Rawling on the Agent-Relative/Agent-Neutral Distinction', *Utilitas*, 13(3), 350–6.

Quinn, Warren S. (1989a), 'Actions, Intentions, and Consequences: The Doctrine of Doing and Allowing', *Philosophical Review*, 89, 287–312.

Quinn, Warren S. (1989b), 'Actions, Intentions, and Consequences: The Doctrine of Double Effect', *Philosophy and Public Affairs*, 18(4), 334–51.

Quong, Jonathan (2009), 'Killing in Self-Defense', *Ethics*, 119(2), 507–37.

Ramsey, F. P. (2010), 'Truth and Probability', in Antony Eagle (ed.), *Philosophy of Probability: Contemporary Readings* (London: Routledge), 52–94.

Rawls, John (1996), *Political Liberalism* (John Dewey Essays in Philosophy; Chichester: Columbia University Press).

Rawls, John (1999), *A Theory of Justice*, rev. edn (Oxford: Oxford University Press).

Raz, Joseph (1986), *The Morality of Freedom* (Oxford: Clarendon Press).

Reichberg, Gregory M., Syse, Henrik, and Begby, Endre (2006), *The Ethics of War: Classic and Contemporary Readings* (Oxford: Blackwell).

Reuben, Anthony (2014), 'Caution Needed with Gaza Casualty Figures', *BBC News Online*, <http://www.bbc.com/news/world-middle-east-28688179>.

Roberts, Adam (2010), 'Lives and Statistics: Are 90% of War Victims Civilians?', *Survival*, 52(3), 115–36.

Roberts, Adam, and Guelff, Richard (2000), *Documents on the Laws of War*, 3rd edn (Oxford: Oxford University Press).

Rodin, David (2002), *War and Self-Defense* (Oxford: Clarendon Press).

Rose, William, Murphy, Rysla, and Abrahms, Max (2007), 'Does Terrorism Ever Work? The 2004 Madrid Train Bombings', *International Security*, 32(1), 185–92.

Rosenbaum, Thane (2014), 'Hamas's Civilian Death Strategy', *Wall Street Journal*, <www.wsj.com/articles/thane-rosenbaum-civilian-casualties-in-gaza-1405970362>.

Ryan, Cheyney (2009), *The Chickenhawk Syndrome: War, Sacrifice, and Personal Responsibility* (London: Rowman & Littlefield).

Schwartz, Yishai (2014), 'Israel's Deadly Invasion of Gaza is Morally Justified', *New Republic*, 21 July, <www.newrepublic.com/article/118788/israels-war-gaza-morally-justified>.

Shane, Scott, and Becker, Jo (2012), 'Secret "Kill List" Proves a Test of Obama's Principles and Will', *New York Times*, <www.nytimes.com/2012/05/29/world/obamas-leadership-in-war-on-al-qaeda.html?smid=pl-share>.

Shaw, Martin (2005), *The New Western Way of War: Risk-Transfer War and its Crisis in Iraq* (Cambridge: Polity).

Shue, Henry (1978), 'Torture', *Philosophy and Public Affairs*, 7(2), 124–43.

Shue, Henry (2010), 'Targeting Civilian Infrastructure with Smart Bombs: The New Permissiveness', *Philosophy and Public Policy Quarterly*, 30(3), 2–8.

Simmons, A. John (1979), *Moral Principles and Political Obligations* (Princeton: Princeton University Press).

Simons, Kenneth (2011), 'When is Negligent Inadvertence Culpable?', *Criminal Law and Philosophy*, 5(2), 97–114.

Slim, Hugo (2007), *Killing Civilians: Method, Madness and Morality in War* (London: Hurst).

Smith, Holly M. (2014), 'The Subjective Moral Duty to Inform Oneself before Acting', *Ethics*, 125(1), 11–38.

Southwood, Nicholas (2013), 'Democracy as a Modally Demanding Value', *Nous*, Online first.

Statman, Daniel (2011), 'Can Wars Be Fought Justly? The Necessity Condition Put to the Test', *Journal of Moral Philosophy*, 8(3), 435–51.

Steinhoff, Uwe (2008), 'Jeff McMahan on the Moral Inequality of Combatants', *Journal of Political Philosophy*, 16(2), 220–6.

Tadros, Victor (2011), *The Ends of Harm: The Moral Foundations of Criminal Law* (Oxford: Oxford University Press).

Tadros, Victor (2014), 'Orwell's Battle with Brittain: Vicarious Liability for Unjust Aggression', *Philosophy and Public Affairs*, 42(1), 42–77.

Temkin, Larry S. (1993), *Inequality* (Oxford: Oxford University Press).

Thomson, Judith Jarvis (1986), *Rights, Restitution, and Risk: Essays in Moral Theory* (Cambridge, Mass.: Harvard University Press).

Thomson, Judith Jarvis (1991), 'Self-Defense', *Philosophy and Public Affairs*, 20(4), 283–310.

UNAMA and AIHRC (2011), *Afghanistan: Annual Report on Protection of Civilians in Armed Conflict 2010*, <http://unama.unmissions.org/Portals/UNAMA/human%20rights/March%20PoC%20Annual%20Report%20Final.pdf>.

UN News Service (2013), 'Ban Strongly Condemns "Totally Reprehensible" Terrorist Act in Nairobi', *UN News Centre*, <www.un.org/apps/news/story.asp?NewsID=45914%20-%20.VHO97Isc-M4>.

US Army (2006), *Counterinsurgency Field Manual* (Washington: United States Army and United States Marine Corps).

US Army (2012), 'Civilian Casualty Mitigation', *Army Tactics, Techniques and Procedures*, 3–37.

Valentino, Benjamin A. (2004), *Final Solutions: Mass Killing and Genocide in the Twentieth Century* (Cornell Studies in Security Affairs; Ithaca, NY: Cornell University Press).

Valentino, Benjamin, Huth, Paul, and Balch-Lindsay, Dylan (2004), ' "Draining the Sea": Mass Killing and Guerrilla Warfare', *International Organization*, 58(2), 375–407.

Valentino, Benjamin, Huth, Paul, and Croco, Sarah (2006), 'Covenants without the Sword: International Law and the Protection of Civilians in Times of War', *World Politics*, 58, 339–77.

Valentino, Benjamin, Huth, Paul, and Croco, Sarah (2010), 'Bear Any Burden? How Democracies Minimize the Costs of War', *Journal of Politics*, 72(2), 528–44.

Walzer, Michael (2006), *Just and Unjust Wars: A Moral Argument with Historical Illustrations* (New York: Basic Books).

Walzer, Michael, and Margalit, Avishai (2009), 'Israel: Civilians and Combatants', *New York Review of Books*, 14 May.

Watts, Barry (1997), 'Ignoring Reality: Problems of Theory and Evidence in Security Studies', *Security Studies*, 7(2), 115–71.

White, Roger (2009), 'Evidential Symmetry and Mushy Credence', in John Hawthorne and Tamar Szabo Gendler (eds), *Oxford Studies in Epistemology* (Oxford: Oxford University Press), iii. 161–86.

Williamson, Timothy (2000), *Knowledge and its Limits* (Oxford: Oxford University Press).

Wolff, Jonathan, and De-Shalit, Avner (2007), *Disadvantage* (Oxford: Oxford University Press).

Wood, Reed M. (2010), 'Rebel Capability and Strategic Violence against Civilians', *Journal of Peace Research*, 47(5), 601–14.

Zimmerman, Michael J. (2006), 'Risk, Rights, and Restitution', *Philosophical Studies*, 128(2), 285–311.

Zimmerman, Michael J. (2008), *Living with Uncertainty: The Moral Significance of Ignorance* (Cambridge: Cambridge University Press).

Zohar, Noam J. (1993), 'Collective War and Individualistic Ethics: Against the Conscription of "Self-Defense" ', *Political Theory*, 21(4), 606–22.

Zohar, Noam J. (2004), 'Innocence and Complex Threats: Upholding the War Ethic and the Condemnation of Terrorism', *Ethics*, 114(1), 734–51.

Index

Printed and bound by CPI Group (UK) Ltd, Croydon, CR0 4YY